# AMAZING & EXTRAORDINARY FACTS

# THE OLYMPICS

# AMAZING & EXTRAORDINARY FACTS

# THE OLYMPICS

## STEPHEN HALLIDAY

David and Charles

A DAVID & CHARLES BOOK
© F&W Media International, Ltd 2012

David & Charles is an imprint of F&W Media International, Ltd
Brunel House, Forde Close, Newton Abbot, TQ12 4PU, UK

F&W Media International, Ltd is a subsidiary of F+W Media, Inc.,
10151 Carver Road, Cincinnati OH45242, USA

Text copyright © Stephen Halliday 2012

First published in the UK and US in 2012
Digital edition published in 2012

Layout of digital editions may vary depending on reader hardware and
display settings.

Stephen Halliday has asserted the right to be identified as author of this
work in accordance with the Copyright, Designs and Patents Act, 1988.

A catalogue record for this book is available from the British Library.

ISBN-13: 978-1-4463-0201-9 Hardback
ISBN-10: 1-4463-0201-6 Hardback

ISBN-13: 978-1-4463-5617-3 e-pub
ISBN-10: 1-4463-5617-5 e-pub

ISBN-13: 978-1-4463-5616-6 PDF
ISBN-10: 1-4463-5616-7 PDF

10 9 8 7 6 5 4 3 2 1

Acquisitions Editor: Neil Baber
Senior Editor: Verity Muir
Senior Designer: Mia Farrant
Production Controller: Kelly Smith

Hardback edition printed in Finland by Bookwell for:
F&W Media International, Ltd
Brunel House, Forde Close, Newton Abbot, TQ12 4PU, UK

F+W Media publishes high quality books on a wide range of subjects.
For more great book ideas visit: www.fwmedia.co.uk

This book is not published in association with the Olympic Committee,
London Organising Committee for Olympic Games (LOCOG) or
endorsed by LOCOG.

# CONTENTS

# INTRODUCTION:
## 'THE GREATEST SHOW ON EARTH'

In Trafalgar Square, London, on Wednesday 27th July 2011 the Belgian President of the International Olympic Committee (IOC), Jacques Rogge, called upon the athletes of the world to assemble in London exactly one year later for the 30th Olympiad of the modern era for what has been described as 'The Greatest Show on Earth'. The Mayor of London, Boris Johnson, speaking shortly afterwards, observed that, since the Olympic venues were ready a year in advance, they should call a snap Olympics there and then and catch the world napping. Boris wasn't quite right. The stadia were built but had to be tried in test events while timing mechanisms and other essential equipment had to be installed. However, it was undoubtedly the case that a previously derelict and much-polluted post-industrial site had been transformed into an Olympic Park and a much-needed green space in a deprived area of East London. This was only the latest miracle in the story of the Olympic Games.

In a sense, by coming to Britain the Modern Olympics were coming home. The ancient games, which ran for over a thousand years, owed their origin to a desire to bring peace to warring Greek city states like Athens and Sparta, and the ancient games had many characteristics in common with the Modern Olympics, including cheating and the adulation of successful competitors. But the abolition of the Games in 393 AD on the grounds that they were pagan meant that they were forgotten for almost 1500 years except in England where the Olympic Games were remembered and celebrated by a motley collection of scholars, con men and a country doctor. Baron Pierre de Coubertin is rightly credited with being the inspiration behind the Modern Olympics. But it is usually forgotten that he drew his inspiration from some unlikely figures including Doctor Thomas Arnold of *Tom Brown's Schooldays* at Rugby School and Dr William Penny Brookes whose 'Much Wenlock Olympics' from 1850 inspired the Frenchman to press ahead with plans to revive the Olympics, beginning at Athens in 1896. The Paralympics were also inspired by an English doctor, Sir Ludwig Guttmann, whose work at the spinal injuries unit at Stoke Mandeville Hospital, Buckinghamshire, led him to conclude that exercise was beneficial to seriously injured people. It is not by chance that the mascots for London 2012 are called 'Wenlock' and 'Mandeville'.

The Modern Olympics are undoubtedly a triumph and have more than justified their motto 'citius, altius, fortius' (Latin for faster, higher, stronger) as records are broken at every games. But they have also been dogged by controversy and involved some very strange people. These range from the man who hitched a lift to win the St Louis Marathon in 1904 (he was caught out); Communist and African dictators who were awarded the Olympic Order for illustrating the Olympic Ideal; drug cheats; and bribery. They have also involved some unusual events including 'The Old Woman's Race for a Pound of Tea' (Much Wenlock, 1850s); live-pigeon shooting (Paris, 1900); the two-handed discus, shot and javelin (Stockholm, 1912); rope-climbing, tumbling and club swinging (Los Angeles, 1932); and medals for art, architecture, literature, painting and music, last awarded in London in 1948.

London thus looks forward to hosting the Olympics for the third time. No other city has achieved this treble though Athens staged the Olympics of 1896 and 1904 and the unofficial 'intercalated games' of 1906. Any account of the Olympics, especially one which focuses on records and other amazing facts as this one does, is dependent upon a variety of sources, many of them contradicting one another.

Stephen Halliday

# THE ANCIENT GAMES

## The Ancient Games
*Holding hands*

A ccording to legend the original Olympic Games were founded by the Greek hero Herakles (Roman Hercules), better known for being obliged to complete twelve apparently impossible tasks, the 'Labours of Hercules' – known as his 'athla' – which is one contender for the origin of the word 'athlete' though one of the rivals is mentioned below.

---

NOT LIKE NEWMARKET
*One of Herakles' labours was that of cleaning the stables of King Augeus. According to this legend Herakles, having completed the task by diverting a river through the 'Augean' stables, was denied his reward by the king whom Herakles then defeated (or possibly killed) in a wrestling match. According to the legend this wrestling match was the first Olympic event.*

---

The first clear record of the games credits them to King Iphitos of Elis, a small state on Greece's Peloponnesian peninsula, south of Corinth. It included the site of Olympia on which, according to an equally convincing legend, a thunderbolt had landed, tossed from Mount Olympus

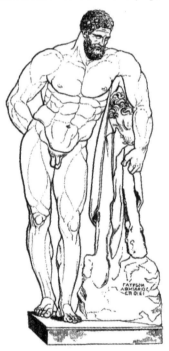

*Herakles*

*Four horse chariot*

by Zeus, king of the gods, in one of his frequent bouts of irascibility. Consequently Olympia contained a shrine and temple to Zeus including a famous statue of the god, one of the seven wonders of the ancient world. It was made of ivory and gold by the most celebrated of Greek sculptors, Phidias, who had also carved the statuary on the Parthenon in Athens. There is, however, some earlier evidence that games involving several cities began as early as 1300 BC under King Aethlius, also of Elis. Some sources suggest that the word 'athlete' owes its origin to King Aethlius rather than to the athla of Hercules. King Iphitos conceived the idea of the games as a means of securing a 'truce', or period of peace, amongst the warring Greek city states. The Greek word is 'ekecheiria' which literally means 'holding hands'. Wars were suspended during the peace and no death penalties were carried out.

THE TROJAN WAR

War and games were strongly associated in Greek culture. According to Homer's Iliad, the Greek hero Achilles, after killing the Trojan prince Hector at the siege of Troy, curbed his wrath by organizing games which included chariot racing, 'hurtful boxing', wrestling, running, hurling a weight, archery and throwing the javelin, events incorporated into the early Olympics which date from about the time of the Trojan War. Greek philosophers like Socrates and Plato rationalized athletic competition as a preparation for military prowess. The games of King Iphitos are first recorded in 776 BC and were preceded by the reading of the 'sacred truce' whose preamble read: 'May the world be delivered from crime and killing and freed from the clash of arms.' Cities which broke the truce

Zeus

were excluded from the games and fined.

## 21ST CENTURY OLYMPIC PEACE
*In July 2004 the Turkish football club Galatasaray of Istanbul and their Greek rivals Olympiakos of Athens signed an 'Olympic Truce' as a sign of goodwill to coincide with the opening of the Olympic Games in Athens. This was a symbolic act of friendship between their two nations and signified the warming of relations following a long period of hostility.*

Throughout the games a fire burned, marking the theft of fire by Prometheus from Zeus, king of the gods. There was no torch in the Ancient Games. As the years passed, the site at Olympia became more elaborate, with the stadium itself surrounded by temples to Zeus and Hera, his wife, a refectory and a workshop for the sculptor Phidias. In 1958 archaeologists found a drinking vessel of the right date at the site engraved with the words 'I am Phidias's'. The site also contained the 'Leonidaion'. This was built by

Leonidas of Naxos in about 350 BC as accommodation for the athletes and may thus be regarded as the first 'Olympic Village', though lavatories were not introduced until two centuries after it was built! In 12 BC the sanctuary of Zeus at Olympia was refurbished following a gift of money from King Herod of Judea, a king not normally associated with charity or with religious tendencies.

At the first Olympic Games there was only one event, a race over a distance known as a 'stade' (about 192 metres, supposedly sixty times the length of Herakles' stride) which was won by a local cook called Coroebus who, running naked as was the custom, thus became the first Olympic champion (despite the claims of Herakles as noted above). A standing long jump of over 7 metres by Chionis of Sparta in the following century would be creditable in the 21st century though he was probably helped by the use of weights held in the hands to propel himself forward. Within two centuries cities from throughout the Greek world were sending competitors, only men of Greek descent being admitted to the

*Olympia*

games. Other events were gradually introduced. In 708 BC the pentathlon was contested, supposedly devised by Jason when he was not searching for the Golden Fleece. In AD 67 at a special event to please Nero, the emperor himself won the chariot race, being the only competitor. Other entrants withdrew and who can blame them? Women were not allowed to participate or even watch the Greek games on pain of death, though presumably the truce meant that the execution would have to wait until the games ended. The only exception was the priestess of the goddess Demeter whose marble seat in its place of honour may still be seen at Olympia. Women could, however, win prizes as a result of owning horses which won the chariot race. There were also separate games for maidens, in honour of the goddess Hera, held at a different time and consisting, it seems, just of a 160 metres foot race. Leonidas of Rhodes was the first multiple medallist; he won the stade (192 metres), the diauos (4 stadia) and the hoplitodromus (24 stadia) in 164, 160 and 156 BC, a record unbeaten in the Ancient Games.

## OLYMPICS AND OLYMPIADS

*From 776 BC the games were held every four years. An 'Olympiad' was a four-year period which began with the celebration of the Olympic Games. This tradition continues, following the revival of the Olympic Games in the modern era, even when the games themselves do not take place because of external influences. Thus the period from 1916 to 1920 remains the 6th Olympiad of the modern era even though the 1916 Olympics did not take place because of the First World War. The term 'Olympiad' does not apply to the Winter Games.*

In 330 BC the Panathenaic stadium, which had hosted games in Athens since 566 BC, was rebuilt in marble in a natural hollow between two hills near Athens by Lycurgus, a Greek politician and pupil of the philosopher Plato. This stadium was restored in the 19th century and used for the first Modern Olympics of 1896. The Ancient Games continued for almost 1,200 years until in 393 AD they were abolished by the Christian Roman Emperor Theodosius who considered them to be a pagan festival. They were always held in Greece except for the year 80 BC when they were moved to Rome by the Roman general and dictator Sulla. Every four years messengers were sent to all the Greek states (including colonies in Spain, Italy, Libya and Turkey) inviting them to send competitors to the games at Olympia, their safe passage being guaranteed by the Olympic Peace. As the Games developed, a system of pre-qualification was introduced. Greek judges would screen those who wished to participate in order to eliminate those who were not of the required standard (like qualifying times for the Modern Olympics). There was even some rudimentary seeding but the usual way of determining contests was for competitors to draw clay tokens from a vessel, each marked with a letter of the Greek alphabet. For example two wrestlers drawing the tokens marked with an alpha would fight each other and others followed this pattern with further letters. One of the athletes from Libya, Eubotas, was so confident of winning a foot race in 408 BC that he commissioned a victory statue beforehand and dedicated it on the day of his victory. The games were attended by thousands of spectators, amongst them the philosopher Plato and the Athenian statesman Themistocles.

*Plato*

## PINDAR

*Plato was one of many scholars of the Ancient World who were drawn to the Olympic Games. On one occasion the mathematician Pythagoras attended, ran into the centre of the arena and bared his right thigh which, he claimed, was made of gold. The Geek poet Pindar wrote several odes to celebrate Olympic achievements including the following:*

*If ever a man strives*
*With all his soul's endeavour,*
*sparing himself*
*Neither expense nor labour to attain*
*True excellence, then must we give*
*to those*
*Who have achieved the goal, a proud*
*tribute*
*Of lordly praise, and shun*
*All thoughts of envious jealousy.*

Alexander the Great was an enthusiastic supporter of the Games, one of his soldiers winning the pentathlon. From about 700 BC the competitions included foot races of varying lengths, wrestling, jumping, throwing (discus, javelin), while Jason's Pentathlon involved running, jumping, discus, javelin and wrestling. In 680 BC 'quadriga' races were introduced, between chariots drawn by four horses like those memorably depicted in the film *Ben Hur* There was a brutal version of boxing in which the hands were covered in hard leather, weighted with metal strips. There were no 'rounds', the contest continuing until one man collapsed, bloody and exhausted, or acknowledged defeat by lifting a finger. There was also 'pankration' (literally 'all force') in which no holds were barred: boxing, wrestling, kicking and strangling were all permitted – but no gouging of the eyes! The Greek word for 'contest' is 'agon' from which our word 'agony' is derived; there was no room for wimps in the sports of the Ancient Greeks! Gymnastics were also introduced. In 396 BC contests

were introduced for trumpet-blowers which would presumably have made the occasion as deafening as the 'vuvuzelas' which became such a prominent feature of the World Cup football tournament held in South Africa in 2010. In accordance with the instructions given to the king of Elis by the sacred oracle at Delphi, victors were garlanded with crowns of wild olives, and such was the prestige associated with victory that they were sometimes awarded pensions by their home cities even though they were competing as individuals and not as representatives of any state. In 412 BC Exainatos of Akragas in Sicily, after triumphs at the games, was welcomed home by 300 chariots which passed through a hole in the city wall since his fellow citizens thought that with such men they needed no walls to protect them. He also received a lifetime exemption from taxation. On the other hand, according to the poet Pindar, those who had performed poorly had to creep home surreptitiously and in one case a boxer called Alis had a mocking statue erected by his opponents 'because he never hurt anyone'.

## CHEATING

*The first recorded cheating was in 388 BC at the 98th games when a boxer called Eupolos of Thessaly was found to have bribed his opponents in order to secure his victory. They were all fined and the money was used to build bronze statues of Zeus which lined the road to the stadium at Olympia.*

# MADE IN ENGLAND: REVIVING THE OLYMPICS

## The Cotswold Olympicks
*Shin-kicking and navvies*

After the abolition of the games in 393 AD by Theodosius they disappeared for 1,200 years from the sporting calendar though they were remembered in the classical syllabuses which dominated English schools and universities. An early reference to the revival of the Olympics in England may be found in the career of Robert Dover. He came from a Catholic family in Norfolk and was a student at Cambridge in 1595 at a time when 'Gog Magog Games' were being held on the Gog Magog hills outside the city. The games were described, humorously, as 'Olympik' at a time when students would have been familiar with the ancient games because the study of the classical world dominated the Cambridge curriculum. Dover was a Catholic sympathizer who left Cambridge without taking a degree to avoid the need to swear the Oath of Supremacy acknowledging Elizabeth I's authority over the English church. He qualified as a barrister at Gray's Inn and in 1610 he settled at Saintbury in Gloucestershire following his marriage to a local widow. In 1612, at Whitsuntide, he organized the 'Cotswold Games' on a hill close to his home near Chipping Campden in Gloucestershire's beautiful Vale of Evesham. Competitors were summoned to the hill (now known as 'Dover's Hill') by a hunting horn and took part in sports such as horse-racing, wrestling, fencing,

throwing the sledge-hammer and
shin-kicking! Dover was acutely
conscious of the Greek heritage
of the games but dismissive of the
Greeks of the 17th century, rather
unfairly since the Greeks were by
that time ruled by the Ottoman
Turks. He expressed his contempt
in verse:

*When Greece frequented active Sport
and Playes,
From other men they bore away the
Prayse;
Their Commonwealth did flourish;
and their Men
Unmatched were for Worth and
Honour then.
But when they once those Pastimes
did forsake
And unto Drinking did themselves
betake,
So base they grew that at this present
day
They are not men, but moving lumps
of clay.*

## SHIN-KICKING
*Shin-kicking was, if anything,
worse than it sounds. Working men,
in hobnail boots or clogs, would
kick each other's shins until one of
them fell to the ground. The skilful
contestant up-ended his opponent in
mid-kick, while he was off balance,
but bouts could last 45 minutes
amidst much blood. The contests are
still held in Chipping Campden but
participants now wear Wellington
boots packed with straw to avoid
serious injury.
The Cotswold Games were briefly
suppressed during the Puritan
ascendancy following the Civil War of
the 1640s but were resumed with the
restoration of Charles II and became
known as the Cotswold Olympicks.
Dover died in 1652 but the games
continued intermittently until 1852
when they attracted controversy
because of the participation of a
number of 'navvies' (labourers) who
were building the nearby Chipping
Campden Tunnel for Isambard
Kingdom Brunel on a branch of
the Great Western Railway. The
behaviour of the navvies offended*

*Isambard Kingdom Brunel*

**some local residents (they were probably spectacularly good at shin-kicking) but the games were revived in 1951 to mark the Festival of Britain and again in 1963, by which time Dover's Hill had passed into the possession of the National Trust.**

By 1636 the 'Cotswold Olympicks' were sufficiently well known to attract a volume of verse published in praise of them. The contributors included Shakespeare's friend Ben Jonson and Shakespeare himself refers to the Olympics in his plays. There has been much speculation about whether Shakespeare knew Robert Dover, a contemporary, and whether the playwright visited the Cotswold Games from his home in nearby Stratford before his death in 1616. In *Henry VI Part III* Shakespeare refers to 'Such rewards as victors wear at the Olympian games'. The Cotswold Games did not pass unnoticed in other quarters.

*William Shakespeare*

# Pierre de Fredi, Baron Coubertin (1863–1937)
*'Anglomaniacs of Sport'*

B aron Pierre de Coubertin was born in Paris on 1 January 1863 and was descended from nobility on both sides of his family, his father tracing his lineage back to medieval Rome. When Coubertin was seven years old, in 1870, France suffered humiliating defeat in the Franco-Prussian War, an experience that prompted many influential

*Baron de Coubertin*

Frenchmen to look across the Channel and ask themselves how the British had managed to build a world-wide empire while France languished. One of those Frenchmen was the writer Hippolyte Taine (1828–93) who visited England and, in 1872, published *Notes sur L'Angleterre* which praised the English system of education, particularly as created by Dr Thomas Arnold at Rugby, and noted approvingly the role of sport in English schools. De Coubertin later read Taine's work which also praised the 'muscular Christianity' of the Reverend Charles Kingsley and other Englishmen whom he associated with the cult of sports and games. Taine's contemporary Edmond Demolins (1852–1907) went further with a book brutally entitled *A quoi tient la supériorité des Anglo-Saxons?* Not all their fellow-citizens were happy with such Anglophile views. Another writer called Pascal Grousset criticized the 'Anglomaniacs of sport' and objected to the formation of a rugby club in Paris called 'Racing Club de France' for its early use of 'Franglais'.

## CHARLES KINGSLEY (1819-75)

*Charles Kingsley is best remembered for his novel* **The Water Babies,** *a moral tale, but he was strongly associated with the promotion of sport and in 1788 formed the 'Committee for the Propagation of Physical Exercise in Education' with himself as its secretary. He had some very strange views on improvements in sanitation and other public health measures which, he feared, would preserve unworthy specimens and lead to the degeneration of the race. He believed that vigorous exercise would 'check the process of degradation which I believe to be going on'.*

In 1875, aged 12, de Coubertin read in a children's magazine, *Journal de la Jeunesse*, a story called 'Aventures de Tom Brown à Rugby', extracted from Thomas Hughes's book *Tom Brown's Schooldays.* In 1883, now aged 20, de Coubertin made the first of a series of annual visits to England and by 1888 had visited ten public schools, Oxford and Cambridge universities, Henley Royal Regatta

and Toynbee Hall in Whitechapel. He was impressed by the central role assigned to sports such as football, rugby, cricket and rowing. In that year he wrote of English education: 'The architecture of their Public Schools is Gothic. Their teaching is somewhat Gothic too but their education is not so at all.' He added, 'Two things dominate in the English system: freedom and sport... hand to hand fighting and punches, especially punches, are not without a certain usefulness in high schools. The English call boxing gloves "the keepers of the peace".' He referred to 'la poussiere Olympique' (Olympic dust) in English education. This flattering view of English education was to bear fruit in the Modern Olympics, but first de Coubertin had to meet Dr William Penny Brookes.

## TOYNBEE HALL

*Toynbee Hall, in Whitechapel, was established in 1884 by the Rev. Samuel Barnett and his wife, Henrietta, both from prosperous backgrounds, to improve the lives of residents of one of London's most impoverished areas, where Jack the*

*Ripper would shortly find his victims. Evening classes, games and food were supplied to those who attended, the early staff including volunteers such as Clement Attlee, the future Prime Minister, whose pragmatic socialism was strongly influenced by his experiences at Toynbee Hall.*

## The Baron and the Doctor
*'The vast Gothic chapel'*

*Dr Thomas Arnold*

Pierre de Coubertin visited many English public schools but, influenced no doubt by his early reading of *Tom Brown's Schooldays*, he was most impressed by Rugby School. Following his visit he wrote a book called *L'Education en Angleterre* in which he wrote that 'organised sport can create moral and social strength'. The hero of the book is Dr Thomas Arnold of Rugby. De Coubertin believed that Arnold, headmaster of Rugby from 1828 to 1842, had promoted the cult of sport within English public schools which underpinned the creation of the British Empire. He visited Rugby

on several occasions and wrote that Arnold 'would not have been an Englishman had he not loved sport' and that he had given 'the precise formula for the role of athletics in education. The cause was swiftly won. Playing fields sprang up all over England.' Thanks to Arnold, de Coubertin believed, sport had shaped England's ascendancy. He recorded his experience at Arnold's tomb in Rugby School chapel, writing: 'How often, at dusk, in the vast Gothic chapel at Rugby, with my eyes fixed on the funeral slab inscribed simply with the name of Thomas Arnold, have I thought to myself that here was the cornerstone of the British Empire?' In contrast, he wrote, in France 'physical inertia was until recently considered an indispensable assistant to the perfecting of intellectual powers.'

But de Coubertin was mistaken about Dr Thomas Arnold's attitude towards sports. *Tom Brown's Schooldays* which had influenced him so much gives an account of life at Rugby during the last years of Arnold's headship when Hughes was a pupil at the school. It contains a fine account of sporting activities, notably a cricket match, and does give the impression that sport was a major feature of the school's life at the time. Thomas Arnold, however, had little interest in sport. He stated that he wanted to create pupils who were Christians, gentlemen and scholars, especially classical scholars, in that order of importance.

## A CLASSICAL EDUCATION

*The values of classical civilization were deeply ingrained in English society in the 19th century, not just in the public schools and universities. The Great Exhibition of 1851 in the Crystal Palace included pictures of 'Victor entering the temple of Zeus' and 'Start of the Running Race'.* **The Spectator** *wrote of the exhibition as 'This Olympic Games of Industry' and early football leagues were given Greek names like the Athenian, Corinthian and Isthmian leagues. The Corinthian Casuals football team was so devoted to the supposed Greek virtue of the gentleman amateur that their players refused to take penalties.*

Dr Arnold didn't mention sport in his writings. A historian of the school later wrote that Arnold's interest in sport was confined to the fact that 'he sometimes stood on the touchline and looked pleased.' Despite his misconceptions about Thomas Arnold and the contributions of others to the Olympic movement,

Pierre de Coubertin is rightly regarded as the moving spirit behind the revival of the games. He died in September 1937 while walking across a Lausanne park close to his home, rather hard up and resentful at what he regarded as the lack of recognition he had received in his native France. Following his death his heart was buried at Olympia on 26 March 1938 in the presence of Crown Prince Paul of Greece. He is commemorated by many statues including one at the headquarters of the IOC in Lausanne, Switzerland, and in 1976 he had a distant planet named after him by a Russian astronomer.

WILLIAM WEBB ELLIS
*A plaque at Rugby School commemorates 'the exploit of William Webb Ellis who, with a fine disregard for the rules of football as played in his time, first took the ball in his arms and ran with it, thus originating the distinctive feature of the Rugby game, AD 1823'. De Coubertin would certainly have known of this claim (rugby was*

*played in France from the 1870s having been introduced to the country by British railway engineers) but there are some serious doubts about whether Webb Ellis ever did any such thing.*

# The Chelsea Olympics
*The 'Baron' and the Carousel ride*

In 1832 the Olympics moved to London where they competed for attention with the Great Reform Bill of that year! This was due to the enterprise of another 'Baron'. This was 'Baron' de Berenger. Born plain Charles Random in the late 18th century, he worked in a humble capacity at a London printing company but then had the good fortune to meet and marry a German widow who styled herself Baroness de Berenger, a title which the new husband assumed, further embellishing it with the style 'Charles Random de Berenger de Beaufain'. A spell in jail for a fraud which involved convincing a number of influential people that Napoleon had died in 1814, a year before Waterloo, did not prevent him from acquiring enough money to buy Cremorne House in the then rural area of London known as Chelsea where he proceeded to construct a number of facilities for sport including riding, shooting and swimming. He wrote books on self-defence which he called 'defensive gymnastics' and called his new facility 'Chelsea Stadium', its motto being 'Volenti nihil difficile' (Nothing is difficult for him who has will). The book was dismissed by one reviewer as 'claptrap' but sold well. There is no record of what happened at the 1832 'Olympic' event but the Baron was sufficiently encouraged to repeat it six years later.

In 1838 the Baron wrote to a journal called *Bell's Life*: 'Permit me to announce directly what to most patrons of the Stadium has been known long since, that I am organizing trials of skill on a grand scale in rifle-shooting, archery, carousel riding, fencing, pistol shooting, gymnastics, sailing, rowing, cricket etc. to commemorate Her Majesty's [i.e. Queen Victoria's] coronation and rewarding the victors with suitable prizes. Accordingly

an entire week will be devoted to daily public contests to be called "The Stadium's first Olympic Week".' Further details of contests, competitors and prizes are not known but we must hope that the 'suitable prizes' would not have been incompatible with the amateur ethos which later came to prevail in the Modern Olympics.

# THE FIRST MODERN OLYMPIAN: WILLIAM PENNY BROOKES AND MUCH WENLOCK

## The First PE Teacher?
*William Penny Brookes and the Much Wenlock Olympics*

If Thomas Arnold was the inspiration, a Shropshire county doctor was the example. William Penny Brookes (1809-95) was born in the small market town of Much Wenlock, Shropshire, to a local doctor and his wife. Their house is

*William Penny Brookes*

still a landmark in the town. William Brookes studied medicine in Paris before taking over his father's practice in 1831 and in 1841 he founded the Much Wenlock Agricultural Reading Society, an early lending library whose aim was to encourage young people to spend their spare time fruitfully by reading and studying. Many such organizations were founded at this time but in 1850 Brookes also founded the 'Wenlock Olympian Class' to 'promote the moral, physical and intellectual improvement of the inhabitants of the town and neighbourhood of Wenlock

and especially of the Working Classes, by the encouragement of outdoor recreation'. The Wenlock Games, first held in October 1850, soon came to include cricket, football, high and long jump, running, hopping races (for under sevens), quoits, chasing the pig, putting the stone and a wheelbarrow race, each event attracting small money prizes. This was soon joined by a race called 'The Old Women's Race for a Pound of Tea' and a handwriting competition for under-sevens. *The Shrewsbury Chronicle* commented approvingly that Brookes' games would be a 'moral armour against the temptations of blacklegs, thimble-riggers [swindlers] etc.' The games soon became very well known and were copied elsewhere. Liverpool began to host Grand Olympic Festivals in 1862, Birmingham in 1867 and Morpeth in Northumberland held its first 'Morpeth Olympic Games' in 1870. Much Wenlock, however, was the dominant force and drew competitors from London, Liverpool and from the German Gymnastic Society in London, as well as 4,000 spectators. Brookes invented the term

'Physical Education' to emphasize that sports had a role in education as well as entertainment and began the practice of awarding a laurel wreath and a medal with an image of Nike, the Greek goddess of victory, thus beginning the custom of awarding medals to victors.

The country doctor foresaw that the Wenlock Games could occupy a national or international stage and in 1859 he was contacted by a number of prominent Greeks living in England, including the Greek ambassador, who were trying to organize Olympic Games in Athens. Brookes sent £10 as prize money and pursued a long correspondence with his Greek contacts to promote the revival of the Ancient Games though at this stage only Greeks could compete in the Athens games, as in the Ancient Olympics. In 1866 Brookes, together with John Hulley of the Liverpool Olympian Association and Ernest Ravenstein of the German Gymnastic Society in London, formed the National Olympian Association and organized the 'National Olympic Games' at the Crystal Palace in Sydenham, South

London. The 440 yards hurdles was won by 18-year-old W.G. Grace who later, after becoming a doctor, became rather well known as a cricketer and who on this occasion abandoned a match for Gloucestershire against Surrey at The Oval in order to compete. In 1877 the 'National Olympian Games' was organized by Brookes in Shrewsbury and King George I of Greece returned the earlier compliment by presenting a silver cup as a trophy. It was inscribed:

*George I, King of the Hellenes*
*For the man who won the Pentathlon*
*at the Modern Olympics of the British*
*at Shrewsbury in August, 1877*

The silver cup is in the Much Wenlock Museum. In return an oak tree was planted at Much Wenlock in honour of the king. The tree still thrives and bears a plaque describing its origins. Brookes lobbied the Greek king, the prime minister and the London ambassador with his proposals for reviving the Olympic Games in Greece but his enthusiasm greatly exceeded that of the Greeks. The long-suffering ambassador, accustomed to the annual avalanche of letters from Brookes on the subject, fended him off with the explanation that the political and financial condition of Greece would not allow it.

In 1889 Pierre de Coubertin appealed through English newspapers for help in reviving the Olympic Games. Dr Brookes contacted him and invited de Coubertin to a meeting of the Wenlock Games in October 1890. He also drew the baron's attention to the relentless campaign that he had been running for years to inspire the Greeks to stage a revival of the games, passing on his correspondence to the younger man who, at 27, was 54 years younger. De Coubertin returned to France inspired by what he had seen, accompanied by a welcoming banner which had been created in his honour. He wrote in *La Revue Athletique* (which he had just founded, modelled on the English magazine *The Athlete*): 'If the Olympic Games that Modern Greece has not yet been able to revive still survive today it is due not to a Greek but to Dr W.P. Brookes.' Dr Brookes' poor health

meant that he was unable to accept an invitation to attend the first meeting of the 1894 Olympic Congress and died four months before the first Modern Olympics in Athens in April 1896. However, de Coubertin was generous in acknowledging his debt to Brookes and in 1994 the President of the International Olympic Committee, Juan Antonio Samaranch, visited Much Wenlock and laid a wreath on the doctor's grave, stating: 'I came to pay tribute and homage to Dr Brookes who really was the founder of the Modern Olympic Games'. William Penny Brookes is remembered by an excellent comprehensive school which bears his name in Much Wenlock. The school hosts some of the events still organized each year by the Wenlock Olympian Society.

# Managing the Olympics
## *The International Olympic Committee*

The International Olympic Committee (IOC) remains the supreme governing body for the Olympic movement and has over

100 delegates including a number of 'honorary' members such as Henry Kissinger whose connection with sport is not entirely clear. It is best thought of as the Olympic Parliament. It chooses the venues for Summer and Winter Games and elects the Executive Board (the 'cabinet') of 15 members which manages the day-to-day affairs of the Olympic movement. Each Olympic Games is organized by an Olympic Games Organizing Committee which in the case of London consists of 18 people. Chaired by Lord Sebastian Coe its members include the Olympic gold medallist Jonathan Edwards, Justin King, chief executive of Sainsbury's and HRH the Princess Royal – herself a former Olympic competitor and member of the IOC.

Henry Kissinger is not the only member of the IOC whose sporting achievements are well concealed. They included the French aristocrat Paul Louis Marie Archambaud de Talleyrand-Périgord, duc de Valençay (1867-1952), a descendant of the noble whose diplomatic skills enabled him to serve (and survive) the regimes of Louis XVI, Robespierre,

Napoleon, Louis XVIII and Louis-Philippe. He became a member of the IOC in 1899. On his mother's side he was descended from the even more exalted Montmorency family. However, Talleyrand is positively common compared with Franz Josef Otto Robert Maria Anton Karl Max Heinrich Sixtus Xavier Felix Renatus Ludwig Gaetan Pius Ignatius, better known as Otto von Habsburg who was born in 1912, third in line to the throne of the Austro-Hungarian Empire, and died in 2011, aged 98, having been elected to the European Parliament in 1979 and having become its longest-serving member. He became a member of the IOC in 1936 and in 1949 was joined by Prince Rainier of Monaco. Sepp Blatter, who has spent time in the news as the somewhat beleaguered President of FIFA, is also a member.

# THE GREEKS JOIN IN!

## An Independent Nation
*Lord Byron and 'Tilting at the Ring'*

The development of the Modern Olympic movement owes much to the emergence of Greece as an independent state. On 25 March 1821 Greece rebelled against the Turkish rule under which the Balkans had been governed since the 14th century, one of the victims of the struggle for independence being the poet Lord

*Lord Byron*

Byron who died at Messolonghi in Greece in 1824. In 1822 Athens was liberated and in 1832 the new Greek state was formed, consisting of a relatively small part of the world of Ancient Greece since it excluded the extensive network of Greek colonies in Turkey, Sicily and North Africa, not to mention Marseilles in France. A German prince, Otto, was foisted as king upon the quite willing Greeks by Britain, France and Russia. After much hesitation Athens, described by Benjamin Disraeli in 1830 as a city without roofs, was chosen as temporary capital of the new nation (they hoped eventually to reclaim Constantinople) and in 1835 it was suggested to the new King Otto that the Olympic Games should be revived and should be held on 25th March, the anniversary of the uprising against the Turks. The idea was attractive to Greek patriots but not to the Greek treasury which had no money. Evangelis Zappas (1800–65) came to the rescue. He began life as a mercenary in the Turkish army but switched sides to join the struggle for independence and later made a fortune from agriculture and shipping. In 1856 he wrote to King Otto offering to fund the revival of the Olympics, with competitors only from Greece and other parts of the Ottoman Empire which included many Greek settlements. In August 1858 a royal decree ordered:

*'National contests to be held every four years and called "Olympics" which have as their purpose to exhibit the products of the activities of Greece especially industry, agriculture and animal husbandry.'*

The wording of the decree reflects the priorities of the bankrupt state which saw the event as a trade exhibition to restore the fortunes of the Greek economy with 'solemn, public athletic games' confined to the third Sunday of the event.

In November 1859 the first Modern Greek Olympics took place in Athens, known as 'The Zappian Games', with the £10 donated by William Penny Brookes as prize money for the winner of 'Tilting at the Ring', a medieval sport which involved a horseman picking up a ring with a lance. It was the biggest

*Evangelos Zappas*

prize on offer but was awarded to the winner of the longest foot race, about a mile in length, with an acknowledgement to 'the Olympic committee of the city of Moudenlok in England'. The race, which took place on a public road, had at one point been impeded by a large fat lady walking her dog. When Zappas died in 1865 he left his large fortune for the Panathenian stadium at Olympia to be restored and used for the four-yearly celebration of the games which continued intermittently. Revival of interest in the games was helped by the fact that from 1875 German archaeologists were excavating Olympia and revealing something of its history. An early visitor to the excavations was the young Oscar Wilde who was punished for arriving late back for term at Oxford. He later wrote, 'I was sent down from Oxford for being the first undergraduate to visit Olympia.' In the years that followed, several 'Olympic' events were held, some of them described as 'elite' games and restricted to wealthy upper-class men. Rope-climbing featured as a popular event, with some games being held in the Panathenian stadium and one, in 1889, in a private gymnasium which resulted in overcrowding and a riot.

In 1862 King Otto abdicated after a series of quite small protests against his authoritarian rule and returned, with relief, to his native Germany. A referendum was held amongst the Greek population who were all agreed that they wanted a king,

*Duke of Edinburgh*

albeit a better one than Otto. The overwhelming favourite was Queen Victoria's second son Alfred, Duke of Edinburgh, who gained 230,066 votes. Second was a member of the Russian royal family with 2,400 votes! However, the one point on which Britain, France and Germany agreed was that the new Greek king should not be British, French or Russian so Prince William of Denmark, who had received six votes, became King of

Greece in 1863 as George I. Britain handed over the island of Corfu, with its famous cricket pitch, to Greece as a kind of welcoming gift to the new dynasty where, 58 years later, it was the birthplace of the present Duke of Edinburgh.

## ROYAL CONNECTIONS

*King George I was assassinated by a madman in 1913 after reigning for 50 years. He was the grandfather of Philip, Duke of Edinburgh who was born in Corfu eight years after his grandfather's death. Born of a Danish father and German mother, he came to England where he was brought up by his uncles, one being Lord Louis Mountbatten. He served in the Royal Navy in World War II, took British nationality and married the future Queen Elizabeth II in 1947. Constantine, former King of Greece, is also descended from the assassinated George I and thus a cousin to Prince Philip.*

# THE MODERN OLYMPICS TAKE SHAPE

## The First Olympic Congress
*Two famous Belgians*

In 1894 de Coubertin organized an international gathering, which he called an 'Olympic Congress' at Paris's medieval university the Sorbonne, then noted for its indifference to sport. The Sorbonne gathering followed a long, hard campaign by de Coubertin to arouse the enthusiasm of his fellow Frenchmen in which, despairingly, he appealed to their sense of patriotism. De Coubertin informed his audience that in the 18th century, 'The England of those days knew only two distractions: doing business more or less honestly and getting drunk more or less completely,' whereas now, 'Wherever they go in the world the English take a tennis racket and a Bible.' Moreover, he told his audience,

'English athletics, gentlemen, only recently began and it is already taking over the world. The universities of Oxford and Cambridge started to associate themselves with it, Thomas Arnold gave the precise formula for the role of athletics in education [as we have seen, this was nonsense], playing fields sprang up all over England...When they left their native land the sons of Albion took the precious recipe with them and athletics flowed into the two hemispheres... Soon the cornerstone of the British Empire had been laid.'

*William Gladstone*

He even quoted Prime Minister William Gladstone as confirming: 'That is right. That is how things happened.' De Coubertin assured his listeners that 'Athens is being reborn on the foggy banks of the Thames' and referred to 'Thomas Arnold who, more than any other Englishman, is responsible for the current prosperity and prodigious expansion of his country.' Arnold would surely have been amazed but de Coubertin had made his point. The gathering ended with the singing of a 'Delphic Hymn to Apollo' which had just been discovered during excavations at the site of the Delphic oracle, set to music by no less a composer than Gabriel Fauré. The British delegation, which was the largest, included the Prince of Wales, the future Edward VII, who was not noted for his athletic prowess. He was one of several Britons who were made Honorary Members of the Congress, along with the future Prime Minister A.J. Balfour and William Penny Brookes who was prevented by illness from attending. De Coubertin urged his audience to 'export runners, rowers and fencers'. The first International Olympic

Committee was formed at this event to run the first Modern Olympics, in Athens in 1896. *The Times* was unenthusiastic, arguing that the attempt to revive the games was futile.

## PRETTY FANNY

*A.J. Balfour was no athlete and his delicacy in manner and appearance earned him the name 'Pretty Fanny'. His contribution to the world of sport was to substitute the name lawn tennis for the game previously known by the unpronounceable sphairistike. He also gave the language the expression 'Bob's your uncle' since he owed his early political elevation to his uncle the Prime Minister, Lord Salisbury, whose name was Robert.*

Following the Congress, Demetrious Vikelas became the first President of the IOC. This came as a surprise to Vikelas. He attended the Congress simply as a representative of the Pan-Hellenic Gymnastic Club and found himself voted into office because de Coubertin thought that the President of the IOC should be from the country that was to host the Olympics, as Athens duly did two

years later. It was at this Congress, moreover, that de Coubertin persuaded his fellow Olympians that the games should be 'ambulatory', moving around the world between cities, rather than permanently based in Greece. Vikelas duly handed over to Pierre de Coubertin after two years, the second Games of the modern era being held in Paris, capital of de Coubertin's native France though de Coubertin soon forgot his belief that the presidency should pass to a citizen of the host nation, keeping the office for himself for 29 years!

The first IOC had 15 members representing 11 countries (Britain, Italy and France each had two members), one of the countries represented being Bohemia and another the Austro-Hungarian Empire. Only nine people have ever held the post of president. No Briton has ever been elected president but two Belgians have held the post, one of them being the current president, Jacques Rogge. Two hundred and five National Olympic Committees now comprise the Olympic movement, with over one hundred representatives sitting on the IOC itself whose members must speak in French or English. The IOC is based at Lausanne in Switzerland and its affairs are managed by an executive committee consisting of the president, four vice-presidents and ten other members who are elected by the full membership. The IOC makes a number of special awards including the 'Pierre de Coubertin Medal' for an athlete who has shown exceptional sportsmanship.

## SALT LAKE CITY BID SCANDAL

*The IOC has sometimes been involved in controversy. In December 1998 it was suggested that members of the IOC had accepted bribes to award the Winter Olympics of 2002 to Salt Lake City, Utah, USA. Ten members of the IOC were expelled and another ten were sanctioned. In 2006 it was suggested that the Japanese city of Nagano had provided excessive hospitality to members of the IOC, the Winter Olympics having been held there in 1998. Similar allegations were levelled against Atlanta after 1996 but supporting documentation could not be found and the allegations were never substantiated.*

# The Olympic Charter
## *From two sentences to five chapters*

The first Olympic Charter was adopted at the 1894 Congress, based on principles set out by William Penny Brookes at Much Wenlock. The 1894 Charter simply stated that: 'The activity of the Olympic movement is permanent and universal. It reaches its peak with the bringing together of the athletes of the world at the great sport festival – the Olympic Games.' The Charter has since become a much more elaborate and lengthy document with five chapters and sixty-one articles. It defines the mission of the Olympic Games; the role of the IOC and of other governing bodies of sports (for example, football, tennis and rugby) and their relationship with the IOC; the role of National Olympic Committees; and the processes by which the host cities will be chosen and the Olympic Games managed. The Charter specifies that all correspondence and debate must be conducted in English or French, an acknowledgement of the central role that both nations played in promoting the creation of the Modern Olympics. The Charter has often struggled to cope with such developments as doping and the conflict between amateurs and professionals.

Difficulties over definitions of amateurism arose from an early stage, and not just in the Olympic movement. William Penny Brookes at Much Wenlock was firmly committed to the amateur ethos, awarding prizes of nominal value as in the case of 'The Old Women's Race for a Pound of Tea' and probably helped to instil this into de Coubertin though the Frenchman's views were ambiguous. For example, in 1894, the year of the Congress, he publicly criticized the amateurism of English rowing at Henley and elsewhere, arguing that its exclusion of working-class athletes was wrong. While he believed that athletes should not be paid to be such, he did think that compensation should be paid to athletes who lost wages when they were competing (though not while they were

training) and would otherwise have been earning money. Following the establishment of a definition for an amateur athlete at the 1894 Congress, he continued to argue that this definition should be amended as necessary and as late as 1909 argued that the Olympic movement should develop its definition of amateurism gradually. At an Olympic Congress in Prague in 1925, the last over which de Coubertin presided, it was agreed that athletes could be reimbursed for up to 15 days of expenses and a competitor had to declare 'on my word of honour that I am an amateur in accordance with the Olympic rules on amateurism'. Anomalies remained. Schools' sports instructors, deriving their income from sport, were allowed to compete while skiing instructors were banned, leading to a boycott of the Winter Olympics by Austria and Switzerland.

## JULES RIMET

*The anomalies that remained as a result of the Prague Agreement on amateurism were not enough to satisfy another Frenchman whose name is as honoured in sport as that of de Coubertin. Jules Rimet never played football (fencing was his preference) but he was convinced that the sport, already played on every continent, would bring people together. He believed that the amateur code of the Olympics unfairly penalized players of the working-class game and, as President of FIFA from 1921 to 1954, abandoned his attempts to incorporate football satisfactorily in the Olympics, pursuing instead the goal of a separate competition which became the first World Cup for the Jules Rimet Trophy in Uruguay in 1928. He thereby created an institution which is the chief rival to the Olympics as an international sporting spectacle.*

*Jules Rimet*

Many injustices were undoubtedly committed in the name of amateurism, beginning with the fate of Jim Thorpe, 'the greatest athlete in the world'. In effect, the strict imposition of the amateur code conferred an advantage on wealthy individuals with private incomes whose training did not have to be interrupted by anything as tiresome as work, like Lord Burghley. The problem became much worse after the 1948 London Games with the entry to the Olympics of Soviet bloc athletes who were professionals in all but name but whose presence was tolerated on pragmatic grounds – the games would have lacked credibility without them. The Americans responded with sports scholarships and the situation remained rife with hypocrisy until 1986 when the requirement for amateur status was removed from the Olympic Charter though certain restrictions remained on professional boxers and wrestlers.

## DOPING

*As amateurism retreated from the Olympics, the problem of performance-enhancing drugs grew since money as well as medals was now at stake. No Olympics is now complete without someone failing a drugs test, the problem being especially acute in weightlifting where steroids are commonly found. As testing and detection methods improve the chemists raise their game to outwit the tests but there have been some spectacular results. Ben Johnson's loss of the gold medal for the 100 metres at Seoul in 1988 was the first really high-profile scandal, followed by the Greek medal hopes Kostas Kenteris and Katerina Thanou who escaped a routine test just before the start of the Athens Olympics of 2004, falsely claiming*

*that they had suffered a motorbike accident. They were banned from the games and later found guilty of perjury, receiving suspended prison sentences. However, the Olympics has managed to avoid the worst excesses of doping scandals of the kind associated with the world of professional cycling.*

*Ben Johnson*

# Orders and Cups
*Dictators, a drunk and a Pope*

*Boris Yeltsin*

B esides gold, silver and bronze medals for athletes the International Olympic Committee also makes awards to people and places whom it considers to be especially deserving. Since 1975 the 'Olympic Order' has been awarded to 'Any person who has illustrated the Olympic Ideal through his/her action, has achieved remarkable merit in the sporting world or has rendered outstanding service to the Olympic cause'. Pope JohnPaul II received the award in 1981 (well, he had been a fine goalkeeper in his younger days and had challenged the authority of some of the nastiest Communist regimes which were in power during his pontificate) but that makes the following winners of the Olympic order all the more puzzling: 1985: Erich Honecker: last Communist dictator of East Germany until overthrown in 1989, his fall being swiftly followed by that of the Berlin Wall of which he was such an enthusiastic supporter; and in the same year the order was presented to that other well-known democrat Nicolae Ceaucescu: deposed and executed in 1989 by the people he had oppressed;
1987: Todor Zhikov: Communist leader of Bulgaria until the collapse of Communism in 1989;
1992: Boris Yeltsin: whose feats of endurance were in the bar rather than on the athletics field;
1995: Robert Mugabe: what is there to add?

The 'Olympic Cup' was instituted by Pierre de Coubertin himself in

1906 for an 'institution or association with a general reputation for merit and integrity that has been active and efficient in the service of sport'. British recipients include:

1907: Henley Royal Regatta;

1915: Rugby School, 'for its immeasurable contribution to sports pedagogy': its influence on de Coubertin has already been noted;

1931: The National Playing Fields Association;

1963: The Commonwealth Games Association.

In 1973 the Cup was awarded to the people of Munich for their fortitude in the face of the tragedy that afflicted the Munich Olympics of the previous year when eleven Israeli athletes and a policeman were massacred by members of Black September, five of whom were also killed. More surprisingly, in 2002 it was awarded to Salt Lake City despite the scandal that arose concerning bribes that were paid in connection with the Winter Games there. On one occasion it has been awarded to a newspaper, the French publication *L'Equipe*.

# ATHENS 1896: THE FIRST MODERN OLYMPICS

## Overspent budgets and dodgy dates, but a triumph nevertheless
*'Twelve foot waves and terribly cold water'*

In 1893 Greece defaulted on its debts (what a surprise!). The Greek Prime Minister, Harilaos Tricoupis, regarded the revival of the Olympic Games as a wasteful frivolity which the country could not afford. He resigned and his successor thought that the Games would help to revive the Greek economy by attracting foreign visitors. Following the creation of the IOC the following year the Greek organizers, under Vikelas, set to work. They tracked down the addresses of foreign sports organizations and sent them invitations; established the rules for entering the competitions and for their conduct; refurbished the venues for each of the events; and identified accommodation in Athens for the competitors and visitors. On 25 March 1896, the 75th anniversary of the beginning of the struggle for independence from Turkey, the first Olympic Games of the modern era were inaugurated by King George of Greece and ran until 15th April.

## JULIUS OR GREGORY?

*According to the rest of Europe the date was actually 6 April. Greece was still following the Julian calendar, created by Julius Caesar, which gives a leap year of 366 days every four years. In 1582 Pope Gregory XIII introduced the more accurate Gregorian calendar which decrees that centenary years will not be leap years unless they can be divided by 400 as well as by 4. So 2000 was a leap year but 1900 wasn't; nor will 2100 be. Catholic Europe adopted the Gregorian calendar after 1582, Britain in 1752 and Greece not until 1923.*

De Coubertin, in a move which was to set a tradition in Olympic budgeting, estimated that the cost of staging the games would be 250,000 drachmas. The true cost was 1,500,000 drachmas! In the absence of any contribution from the empty Greek treasury the organizers had raised money through the sale of commemorative stamps and medals and from private donors, the most generous being a wealthy Greek businessman called Georgios Averoff who had paid to complete the refurbishment of the Panathenian stadium in Athens. This stadium, dating from the 6th century BC, had hosted the Panathenian Games in honour of the goddess Pallas Athene; these games were almost as old as the Olympics themselves. The stadium was brought out of retirement for the Modern Olympics.

To mark the Games' opening, a Greek ode was composed and declaimed by George Robertson, a former pupil of Winchester College who had met de Coubertin when the Frenchman visited the school in his examination of the English educational system ten years earlier. A crowd of 80,000 (considerably greater than the population of Athens at the time) saw the first

Olympic title for over 1,500 years won by James Connolly of Boston, Massachusetts with a triple jump of 13.71 metres. He was followed by a Greek youth called Zopyros of Athens who won the boys' pankration, a mix of boxing and wrestling that was a good deal less brutal than its ancient equivalent. The discus competition presented all sorts of problems and surprises. An American commentator who watched English competitors struggling with the unfamiliar object commented that 'The efforts of the English novices was ludicrous,' and he was perhaps fortified by the knowledge that his compatriot Robert Garrett of Princeton won the event, having picked up a discus for the first time the night before the games began. Many of the contestants were visitors who happened to be in the Athens area when the games were staged. One of them was Jack Boland, later an MP for Kerry, who was by chance visiting Athens on holiday and decided to enter the tennis competition to secure a court on which to play. He won! In a touching display of respect for regal authority a French sprinter ran in white gloves

because he was in the presence of the Greek king. They didn't help his cause; he didn't win the race. Besides the athletic events commonly associated with the Ancient Games there were competitions in fencing, wrestling, weightlifting, cycling (then a new pastime using primitive vehicles), tennis and swimming. The fencing competition included a special class for fencing masters who were, in effect, professionals and were distinguished in this way from the true amateurs, a strange departure from the amateur ethos that de Coubertin favoured. The most unfortunate would-be athlete was an Italian runner, Carlo Airaldi, who, having walked most of the way from Milan to Athens, was declared ineligible because he was deemed to be a professional. If only he had been a fencer! The swimming competitions were held in the chilly waters of the Aegean Sea. The Hungarian winner, Alfred Hoyos Guttmann, described it: 'I won ahead of the others with a big lead, but my greatest struggle was against the towering twelve-foot waves and the terribly cold water.' He did better than the American

*Spiridon Louis*

the shore. The Ancient Games never included swimming. Victors received a silver medal and crown of olive leaves and runners-up a copper medal and laurel crown. The 1896 games also included pistol shooting, at which de Coubertin was French champion.

The Greeks had to wait until the final day for their first athletic title when Spiridon Louis, variously described as a shepherd or a water-carrier, won the Marathon, the most prestigious event, in a time of 2 hours, 58 minutes 50 seconds. Spiridon was in fact a former soldier from a prosperous family who, following his victory, received numerous gifts (gold watches, a Singer sewing machine, life-time free rail travel) and proposals of marriage. More practically, he was granted the concession to supply water from his village of Maroussi to the growing city of Athens which provided him with a comfortable living. He was followed home by two more Greeks, one of whom was disqualified when a Hungarian runner complained that the third man home had travelled some of the distance in a horse and carriage, an offence which nearly won the

Gardner Williams who, having crossed the Atlantic to compete, dived into the chilly waters, surfaced, cried, 'I'm freezing' and headed back to gold medal eight years later at St Louis. Women were not allowed to participate in the games, as in ancient times, but one determined young Greek woman, Stamata Revithi, ran the Marathon course the day after the men, finishing in 5 hours 30 minutes though she was not allowed to enter the Panathenian stadium. During the Games the former Prime Minister, Tricoupis, who had been so hostile to the whole scheme, died in some comfort on the French Riviera.

At Athens 14 nations were represented by 245 competitors, all male.

## A TRUE MARATHON

*The Marathon was not included in the Ancient Olympic Games. It was introduced to the Olympics of 1896 at the suggestion of a Frenchman, Michel Breal, who presented as a trophy a cup which still exists. Pierre de Coubertin embraced the idea because he wanted an event which would reflect the glories of Ancient Greece. It was based on the exploits in 490 BC of the Greek runner Pheidippides who, having run 150 miles from Athens to Sparta to summon help against the invading Persians, returned to take part in the Battle of Marathon at which the Persians were defeated. He then ran the 26 miles to Athens to announce the victory and collapsed, dying after uttering the words 'We have won.' One wonders why they couldn't have found him a horse.*

*Pheidippides*

## Paris 1900
*Duck when you see the discus thrower*

The Greeks had assumed that the Modern Olympics, like the Ancient Games, would find a permanent home in Greece but Pierre de Coubertin had always intended that they would become an international event and, through deference to his role in reviving the games, those of 1900 were held in his native Paris to coincide with the 'Universal Exposition' held in the French capital that year.

## WHEN IN GREECE …

*Further attempts to secure the Olympics permanently for Greece were made by the Greek Prime Minister Constantine Karamanlis in the 20th century. In 1976, in the face of boycotts and financial pressures at the Montreal Games, he argued that a site in Greece, possibly Olympia itself, would be financially more sustainable and less sensitive politically. He was turned down by the IOC and again when he tried in 1980 on the same grounds following the Moscow Olympics. Too many had by then recognized global marketing opportunities in the Olympics.*

The decision to combine the games with the Exposition was a mistake since the task of organizing the Games was taken over by the committee responsible for the Exposition who regarded the Olympic Games as a sideshow to the main event, little more than a

*Paris 1900, USA Olympic Team*

device for encouraging people to attend the Exposition itself. Cricket, croquet, football, rugby, rowing, golf, equestrian sports and sailing were introduced for the first time. There was no proper stadium, just a grass enclosure in the Bois de Boulogne where the long jumpers had to dig their own pit. The area was not without its hazards since the 1896 discus champion sent all three throws into the admittedly sparse Paris crowd. Many competitors appear to have believed that they were competing in the Universal Exposition rather than the Olympics. No medals were awarded though cups and other trophies were presented to winners.

## GOLD TEETH?

*The American athlete Alvin Kraenzlein took first place in the 60 metres sprint, the 110 metres and 200 metres hurdles and the long jump – four first places in athletic events which were not matched until Jesse Owens in 1936. The feat has never been surpassed at one Games. He later became a dentist.*

Despite the chaotic organization there were some notable firsts. Women were allowed to compete for the first time, in archery, tennis and sailing despite the misgivings of de Coubertin who felt that their participation was a departure from the traditions of the Ancient Games (as it certainly was). Athletics were still firmly barred to them. The first female title winner was Charlotte Cooper of Great Britain in tennis and Constantin de Zubiera from Haiti became the first black athlete to compete, winning a trophy for France in the tug-of-war. There was also the first flickering of opposition to competing on the Sabbath which would be made famous by the Scotsman Eric Liddell at the 'Chariots of Fire' Games of 1924. Oddly it involved an American of Jewish descent called Myer Prinstein who was a student at the Methodist University of Syracuse. Despite refusing to compete in the finals of the long jump on the Sunday he gained second place by virtue of his qualifying jump in the first round on the Saturday (which was, of course, the Jewish Sabbath). Alvin Kraenzlein won the gold by a centimetre to the fury of Prinstein who had thought that Kraenzlein would also refuse to compete on the Sabbath. He was with difficulty restrained from assaulting the four-times winner. Britain won the football competition, the successful team being Upton Park Football Club, not to be confused with West Ham United, formed the same year, whose stadium is Upton Park.

## YOUNGEST EVER

*A record unlikely to be broken was set in rowing. When the cox for the Dutch coxed pairs crew failed to arrive on schedule they enlisted the help of a young French boy variously described as being seven or ten years*

*old. Records at the time were poor*
*and do not enable a clear judgement*
*to be made but it appears that his*
*name may have been Marcel Depaillé*
*though there are no clear records to*
*confirm this.*

*In Paris 19 nations were represented*
*by 1,066 male and 12 female*
*competitors.*

## St Louis, Missouri, 1904
### A bad case of cramp

*St Louis, 1904*

The remoteness of St Louis, Missouri, long before the days of air travel, ensured that the number of participants was little more than half those of Paris four years earlier. Once again the opportunity was taken to combine the Olympics with another event, the 'St Louis World's Fair' which was held to celebrate the 100th anniversary of the Louisiana Purchase when President Thomas Jefferson bought 828,800 square miles of land from France for 15 million dollars. The territory now encompasses all or part of fifteen US States, surely the shrewdest real estate deal in history. Eighty-five percent of the competitors were from the United States itself though the Canadians did manage to scrape together 11 players for a football team who duly lost to the only other competitors, the USA. Both the winners and runners-up in the water polo event represented the USA. The rowing competition, over a course of 2,400 metres (the current event is over a course of 2,000 metres) required the crews to execute a turn halfway through the race while Archie Hahn, representing the USA, won the 200 metres event despite starting 0.914 metres behind the other runners for a false start. This strange calculation occurred because the Americans insisted on using imperial measurements (yard, feet and inches) and 0.914 metres was one yard.

The most extraordinary event was the Marathon. Fred Lorz of the USA, overcome by cramp, flagged down a passing truck which gave him a lift, enabling Lorz to wave to other runners as he passed them. When the truck itself suffered a breakdown after ten miles, Lorz, refreshed, resumed his run and entered the stadium

*Fred Lorz*

well before any other competitor, sending the spectators into a frenzy of patriotic excitement. Alice Roosevelt, daughter of the President Theodore Roosevelt, was about to hand Lorz the trophy when his irregular approach to the event was drawn to her attention, at which point cheers were replaced by loud booing. After an interval the second arrival was that of Tom Hicks, a British-born US citizen who was himself dazed and barely aware of his surroundings, having been dosed with strychnine to dull the pain of competition, a reasonably common practice at the time and not illegal. Hicks duly received the trophy to more subdued applause.

At St Louis 13 nations were represented by 681 male and 6 female competitors.

## Athens, 1906
### *The Intercalated Games*

After the poor organization at Paris and the falling numbers at St Louis, de Coubertin, as chairman of the IOC, was anxious to give some fresh impetus to the games and proposed an extra event, known as the 'Intercalated Games' in Athens in 1906. Every effort was made to emphasize the importance of the event. According to a contemporary account left by a member of the British fencing team, Sir Theodore Cook, 'The British athletes were led by their official chief and representative, Lord Desborough, in a top hat and frock coat' and the games were attended by King Edward VII and Queen Alexandra, the only occasion on which a British monarch has attended Olympic Games overseas. Although not usually recognized as true Olympics these Games were the first to have an 'Olympic Village' for the athletes in the form of the 'Zappeion'. The building had been constructed in the 1870s with a view to the eventual revival of the games, the money having been provided by Evangelis Zappas. Zappas did not live to see the completion of the building, though his head is buried beneath the statue of him which stands outside the building. The 'Zappeion' was used as the fencing hall for the 1896 Olympics before serving as

*Edward VII*

accommodation for the 1906 games. It remains an attractive feature of Central Athens to this day and is used for conferences and exhibitions.

### JOIN THE CLUB

*In 1981 the Zappeion was the location of another important event in the history of Greece when it was used for the signing of the documents which marked Greece's accession to the European Union. It also served as the press centre for the 2004 Games.*

A new version of the pentathlon was introduced in the 1906 games consisting of the 192 metre 'Stade'; the standing long jump; the discus; the javelin; and wrestling. However, the most curious spectacle of the games was provided by William Sherring of Canada who won the Marathon while wearing a trilby hat to protect himself from the sun! He was duly presented with a bouquet of flowers and a small goat which he led back to his quarters, no doubt wondering what to do with it. Lord Desborough, leader of the British representatives, was a member of the British fencing épée team which was runner-up to the French team. Alongside him in the team was Sir Cosmo Duff-Gordon, a Scottish baronet who was to achieve distinction of a different, and unsought, kind six years later. He, his wife and servant were rescued on one of the *Titanic's* few lifeboats which, though holding only 12 out of a maximum of 40 places, declined to pick up other survivors from the icy water. He was booed in New York and ostracized in London for his apparent cowardice. The Intercalated

*William Sherring*

Games of 1896 in Athens are not regarded as 'official Olympics' but they helped to re-establish the Games after the comparative fiascos of Paris and St Louis. Twenty nations were represented by 833 male and 20 female competitors. They kept the Olympic flame burning for the 1908 Olympics at which the number of competitors exceeded the combined total of Athens, Paris and St Louis.

# THE OLYMPICS GATHER PACE

## When not in Rome...
*London to the Rescue*

The London Olympics of 1908 should have been the Rome Olympics. By 1906 the Italian authorities were well behind with their preparations so when Vesuvius conveniently erupted the same year the Italians announced that Rome was 'off'. London stepped into the breach in the person of the redoubtable Lord Desborough, he of the top hat and frock coat in Athens two years earlier. He was an Oxford rowing Blue who had participated in the famous race's only dead heat in 1877, had climbed the Matterhorn and swum across the base of Niagara Falls, so mounting the Olympic Games was child's play. He quickly persuaded the organizers of the Franco-British Exhibition of 1908 to build its facilities in such a way as to accommodate an athletics track, a swimming pool and cycle track.

It was completed in ten months at a cost of £75,000 and could hold 130,000 standing spectators. Its ugly concrete walls earned it the name 'White City'. Desborough died in 1945, one of the few people to have read his own (flattering) obituary which had been published in error by *The Times* in 1920!

*Lord Desborough*

*London 1908 Opening Ceremony*

## WHITE CITY

**Following the 1908 Olympics the White City stadium was used for a variety of events including athletics, speedway and pop concerts. It was demolished in 1985 and part of the site was used to build a new site for BBC Television. In 2008 most of the rest of the site was used to accommodate the Westfield Centre, the largest shopping centre in London.**

Twenty-two nations sent 2,035 competitors (twice the previous record) to compete in 107 events – another record. Thirty-six of the competitors were women, despite the opposition of de Coubertin. One of them was the formidable Charlotte 'Lottie' Dod (1871-1960). Having won the Wimbledon Ladies Singles title at the age of 15 (still a record), represented England at hockey and won the women's national golf championship, she turned to archery and won an Olympic silver medal in 1908. Her pedigree helped. Her ancestor, Sir Anthony Dod, had commanded the English archers at Agincourt and her brother, Willy, won the gold medal in the men's event, making them the first brother/sister Olympic medallists. Lottie died in 1960 while listening to a radio broadcast of the Wimbledon championships. At the London Games the organizers insisted on translating metric measurements into imperial ones so the winner of the 100 metres was announced as the winner of the 109.3 yards event! The London Games were the first at which the first three in events all received gold, silver and bronze medals (rather than some receiving diplomas) and the only Games at which Britain won most medals, with 146 medals in total, including 56 golds, three times the haul of the USA in second place.

One of the golds was for football, these being the first games in which representative national teams (rather than club teams) competed. An England amateur team beat Denmark two-nil in the final with a British referee officiating. Britain also swept the board in rowing events which were held at Henley.

## NO TROUBLE COUNTING THE GOALS

*The defeated Danish team included the eminent Danish mathematician Harald Bohr (1887–1951) whose brother was the even more famous Niels Bohr, winner of the Nobel Prize for Physics. Not many families can boast a Nobel prizewinner and an Olympic silver medallist in the same generation.*

The London Games were not without controversy. At the opening ceremony, performed by King Edward VII on 13th July, the team from Finland refused to bear a flag when told that they would have to march under the standard of Tsarist Russia. Irish competitors, told they would have to compete for Britain, withdrew in protest. The USA, whose flag had been accidentally omitted from those flying at the stadium, refused in protest to 'dip' the Stars and Stripes as they passed the royal box. The Swedish team, whose flag had also been overlooked, declined to participate in the opening ceremony at all. Another argument with the Americans arose when one of their team was judged to have obstructed an English athlete in the final of the 400 metres and was disqualified. Following American protests the race was re-run but the Americans, William Robbins and John Taylor, boycotted the event so the Englishman, Wyndham Halswelle, jogged alone around the track for his gold medal, the only 'walk over' in Olympic history. Another American, Forrest Smithson, won the 110 metres hurdles while protesting against the final being held on a Sunday by carrying a Bible, though a photograph of him carrying the book appears to have been staged some time after the event.

## MEDLEY RELAY

*Medley relays are normally associated with swimming but John Taylor, having boycotted the re-run 400 metres final, became the first black American to win a gold medal when he ran the 400 metre leg in the 1600 metres medley relay team. Two runners called Hamilton and Cartmel each ran 200 metres, Taylor ran the 400 metre leg and the final 800 metre leg was run by Mel Sheppard, a total of 1600 metres. This was the first Olympic relay event, run by touch, without batons, and the last 1600 metre medley relay.*

Following the 400 metres controversy the Americans complained that their treatment was 'cruel, unsportsmanlike and unfair'. At a dinner to mark the games George Robertson, who had composed and recited the 'Olympic Ode' at the first games of 1896, called the American team management 'liars and no sportsmen'! Moreover, criticisms were sufficiently severe for the organizers to produce a document entitled 'Replies to Criticism of

the Olympic Games' which is as tedious as its title suggests. In future, however, all officials were appointed by international bodies rather than the host country to avoid the appearance of bias. The Marathon fell on the final day of competition and at the request of the king it began on the lawns of Windsor Castle so that his grandchildren (including the future Edward VIII and George VI) could watch. The race was started by Princess Mary of Wales, soon to become Queen Mary when her husband, George V, succeeded Edward VII in 1910. The distance to the finish was 26 miles 385 yards which from that time was established as the standard distance for the Marathon. At previous games the distance had been set at 40 kilometres (25 miles). First to enter the stadium was an Italian confectioner called Dorando Pietri who, in white vest and bright crimson shorts, was greeted by a deafening roar from the excited crowd. In his exhausted state Pietri ran the wrong way round the track. Guided by others (one of whom may have been Conan Doyle, author of *Sherlock Holmes*, who was certainly

*Dorando Pietri*

at the trackside as a journalist) Pietri was led to the finishing line and, in accordance with the rules, disqualified, the gold medal going to Johnny Hayes of the USA. Pietri's habit of gargling with wine to refresh himself as the race progressed may have helped to account for his confused condition. The Americans were again enraged when the Italian flag was mistakenly hauled to the top of the flagpole above the Stars and Stripes. The following day Queen Alexandra presented Pietri with a gold cup as a consolation prize. Since his name had been wrongly entered in the contest as 'P. Dorando' it was

this name that was inscribed on the trophy.

The 1908 Games were the first to feature 'Winter' events, with four figure-skating competitions. The tennis competition was held at Wimbledon and sailing on the Clyde, the only time that an Olympic event has been staged in Scotland. Another legacy of the London Games did not endure. During the Games the President of the Royal Academy, Sir Edward Poynter (1836–1919) persuaded the IOC that in future there would be medals for artistic activities including architecture, sculpture, music, painting and literature. In 1912 the gold medal for literature was awarded, with commendable diplomacy, to Pierre de Coubertin for his poem 'Ode to Sport' which has, however, failed to win a lasting place in the annals of literature. These awards continued up to the 1948 Games, again in London, after which they were discontinued on the grounds that most of the entries were from professional artists, contrary to the amateur ethos of the Olympics.

At the London Games 22 nations

were represented by 1,999 male and 36 female competitors.

## THE MOST IMPORTANT THING

*The first Olympic motto was adopted by de Coubertin from a sermon preached by the Bishop of Pennsylvania during the London Games of 1908: 'The most important thing is not to win but to take part.' It is now described as the Olympic creed. The present motto citius, altius, fortius (Latin for faster, higher, stronger) was adopted at the Paris Games of 1924, having been previously suggested to de Coubertin by his friend Henri Didon, a Dominican priest who was also an enthusiastic sportsman.*

# Stockholm 1912
*'The Greatest Athlete in the World' – disqualified!*

The Stockholm Games of 1912 were the first to be organized upon recognizably modern lines. London had been the greatest success to date but controversies had arisen over the use of British referees and officials and the bias this supposedly introduced. At Stockholm, for the first time, officials were appointed by the governing bodies of their sports including FIFA which had been created in Paris in 1904 (the Football Association of England joining later) and which chose the football referees for Stockholm. The football tournament was won by Great Britain who, as in the London Olympics, beat Denmark by two goals in the final, who this time played without Harald Bohr. There were, however, some other notable participants. Lieutenant George S. Patton of the USA came fifth in the pentathlon competition,

*Stockholm 1912, Opening Ceremony*

later achieving distinction and a degree of notoriety as a World War II general.

*George S. Patton*

## TWO WARS AND A SLAP IN THE FACE

*In World War II Patton fought two wars, one against the Germans and the other against his fellow generals, a long-running feud with the equally vain Montgomery being especially prominent. He achieved notoriety for slapping the face of an American soldier who was in hospital suffering from shell-shock after the invasion of Sicily, and was himself killed in a road accident in Germany in December 1945.*

The American Ralph Craig won the 100 metres and 200 metres despite being responsible for three of the seven false starts in the two races. Under later rules he would have been disqualified. Oscar Swahn of Sweden at 65 set a new record as the oldest Olympic competitor to that date, winning gold and silver medals for shooting. But he wasn't finished and would break his own record eight years later in Antwerp and still holds the record as the oldest winner of a gold medal. Extraordinary records were set in the wrestling competition. In the light-heavyweight division the final was abandoned after nine hours without a result, each contestant being awarded a silver medal. In the middleweight division they showed more stamina, the contest being won by an Estonian after eleven hours forty minutes.

The most extraordinary athlete to compete at Stockholm, and perhaps at

*Jim Thorpe*

any Olympics, was Jim Thorpe (1888–1953), of mixed Caucasian and Native American ancestry whose 'Red Indian' name was Wa-Tho-Huk or 'Bright Path'. He won the decathlon and pentathlon by embarrassing margins and when he was presented with his medals at the closing ceremony (as was then the custom) the King of Sweden informed him, 'You, Sir, are the greatest athlete in the world', to which Thorpe replied 'Thanks, King.' A ticker-tape parade

on Broadway followed. However, the adulation was short-lived. In January 1913 an article in the *Worcester Telegram*, a Massachusetts newspaper, claimed that as he had played minor league baseball for trivial sums in 1909 and 1910, he was a professional. Minor league baseball was common practice amongst college students who preserved their amateur status by adopting pseudonyms. Thorpe's failure to do this was fatal. His name was deleted from the Olympic record though, to their credit, the runners-up to Thorpe in the competitions he had won refused to accept the gold medals, believing they had been fairly won by Thorpe. In the USA his fellow-citizens were less sympathetic, much of the criticism of him making disparaging reference to his Native American ancestry. After his disgrace he signed for the New York Giants baseball team and also played professional basketball and American football, one of his opponents in the last of these being the future general and president Dwight D. Eisenhower who described Thorpe as 'the greatest football man I've seen'. The end of his athletic career coincided with the onset of the Great Depression and Thorpe's life descended into penury and alcoholism. He died in 1953 of a heart attack. In 1982 he was pardoned by the IOC and his confiscated medals were returned to his family, later being stolen from a museum. He is remembered by Jim Thorpe, Pennsylvania, the small town which took his name after his death, a place he never visited.

At Stockholm 28 nations were represented by 2,382 male and 55 female competitors.

# RECOVERING FROM WAR

## Antwerp 1920
*A Sculler, a Princess and a Tug-of-War*

The 1916 Olympics, scheduled for Berlin, were a casualty of World War I and such was the hostility towards Germany and its allies that all four – Austria, Hungary, Turkey and Germany itself – were excluded from the 1920 Games

which should have been held in Budapest but were transferred to Antwerp. For the first time the Olympic Oath and the Olympic Flag were used. The Olympic Oath, written by de Coubertin himself, is taken by an athlete of the host country and was first uttered by Belgian fencer Victor Boin at the Antwerp Games: 'In the name of all competitors, I promise that we shall take part in these Olympic Games, respecting and abiding by the rules that govern them, in the true spirit of sportsmanship, for the glory of sport and the honour of our teams.' As the oath is spoken the athlete holds a corner of the Olympic flag which bears five interconnected rings in blue, yellow, black, green and red on a white background. The first flag was presented to the IOC by the city of Antwerp and is doubly symbolic. The colours were chosen because every national flag contains at least one of them; and the five rings represent the earth's five principal inhabited continents.

As so often the USA was foremost amongst the medal winners though they were not a happy team. The world, especially Europe, was still recovering from the Great War and the Americans arrived on a rusty old freighter and were accommodated in schools. They did, however, have some remarkable competitors. A gold medal for diving was won by Aileen Riggin, four feet eight inches tall and aged 14 years 119 days. Ethelda Bleibtrey, who had taken up swimming to help her recovery from polio, won three gold medals despite having been arrested in 1919 for 'nude swimming', having removed her stockings at a pool where it was forbidden to bare 'the lower female extremities for public bathing'. The team from Finland were much happier because, for the first time, they were allowed to compete under their own flag rather than that of Tsarist Russia which had disappeared with the Bolshevik Revolution. They were even happier when, at his first Olympic Games, the great Paavo Nurmi won the first three of his nine gold and three silver medals which he was to win over three Olympics. Nurmi made his training runs in army boots to strengthen his leg muscles and was a pioneer in the use of interval training:

short sprints immediately followed by longer runs at medium pace. The silver medal in the 1500 metres went to Philip Noel-Baker (1889-1982) of Great Britain. Of Quaker stock, Noel-Baker was later to become a Labour MP, a minister in the wartime coalition government under Churchill and, in 1959, winner of the Nobel Peace Prize for his lifelong campaign against war in the League of Nations and the United Nations. Oscar Swahn once again competed for Sweden, now setting a new record for longevity at 72 but he wasn't quite finished yet!

*The Finnish flag*

## TUG OF WAR

*The Antwerp Games were the last Olympics in which the tug-of-war was contested, the gold medal being taken by a team from Britain's smallest police force, the City of London Police (not to be confused with the Metropolitan Police, Britain's largest, from whom the City Police maintain their independence). The City Police are thus the reigning Olympic champions.*

triumph was that of the rower John B. ('Jack') Kelly who won the single and double sculls. Earlier in the year he had been refused entry to the Henley Royal Regatta on the grounds that he was a bricklayer, not a gentleman, whose horny-handed means of earning a living would presumably have given him an advantage over the gentlemen amateurs who ran the regatta. The regatta's rules excluded anyone who was 'by trade or employment for wages a mechanic, artisan or labourer'. In fact he was

*Tug of War*

Another prominent name was that of Suzanne Lenglen who won gold medals for tennis in the ladies' singles and mixed doubles and won six Wimbledon singles titles in her career. However, the most extraordinary (and for Great Britain most embarrassing)

*Grace Kelly*

a very successful builder who built much of Philadelphia and became a self-made millionaire. At Antwerp he won the first two of his three gold medals. His son, John Kelly Jr., was allowed into Henley in 1947, winning the Diamond Sculls, and won a bronze medal at the Melbourne Olympics of 1956. Jack Kelly's daughter was the film star Grace Kelly who, as Princess Grace of Monaco, presented the prizes at Henley in 1981, the year before her death. At Antwerp 29 nations were represented by 2,543 male and 64 female competitors.

# Paris 1924: Chariots of Fire
*But not in Cambridge*

Many will have seen the 1981 Oscar-winning film *Chariots of Fire* which celebrates the British victories in the Paris Olympics of 1924. Harold Abrahams, who weighed three pounds at birth and was not expected to survive for very long, was the first European to win the 100 metres while Eric Liddell, competing in the unfamiliar 400

metres event because he wouldn't run on a Sunday in the heats for the 100 metres, won the gold medal for the longer distance. The film exaggerates the anti-Semitism that Abrahams suffered but is correct in emphasizing his use of a famous professional coach, Sam Mussabini, who taught him the 'dip' finish which he pioneered and is still used. Abrahams later recalled that there was no medal ceremony, his gold being sent to him later by post! The film doesn't mention that Abrahams criticized later athletes for more moderate 'professional' approaches to their sport. He didn't approve of Roger Bannister's use of Christopher Chataway and Chris Brasher as pacemakers in Bannister's successful attack on the sub-four minute mile, for example. Abrahams later became a respected athletics administrator but felt that his achievements as a sprinter were forgotten, never gaining the knighthood he thought he deserved. He remained obsessively concerned with time, carrying two stop watches with which to time himself going to the lavatory or for a walk! Abrahams later became secretary to

*Abrahams and the Duke of York*

the National Parks Commission and designated both the Lake District and Dartmoor as National Parks. Eric Liddell remained a devout Christian and died in a Japanese internment camp in World War II having been captured while working in China as a missionary.

## LONGER AND HIGHER
*The 1924 Paris Games were the first at which a black athlete won an individual gold medal, this being William De Hart Hubbard of the USA in the long jump. In the high jump Harold Osborn of the USA courted controversy by adopting a new style of jumping, the 'Western Roll', which enabled him to press the bar back against the uprights as he crossed it. This was legal at the time but soon ceased to be so.*

But *Chariots of Fire* is also remembered for the 'Great Court Run' in which, according to the film, Harold Abrahams succeeded in running round the Great Court of Trinity College, Cambridge, in the time it took for the courtyard's clock to strike twelve. This is not easy. The distance is approximately 367 metres and the clock, which strikes twice, takes 43 to 45 seconds, dependent upon the temperature. Moreover the run involves four sharp corners and cobbles. It takes place in October each year on the day after the 'Matriculation Dinner' when new students are admitted to the university. It is not surprising that it has only been done twice: once by Lord Burghley in 1927 and once by second-year undergraduate

*Cambridge*

Sam Dobin in 2007. Burghley won the 400 metres in the Amsterdam Olympics of 1928. Sebastian Coe tried to complete the run for charity in 1988 and failed by 1.6 seconds. So what of Harold Abrahams? He attended Cambridge University but never did the Great Court Run! And the Great Court Run in *Chariots of Fire* was not run at Trinity College. The college authorities would not allow the filming to take place there, allegedly because they thought that it would project an 'elitist' image that would deter students from applying to the university. So where did they film it? Eton College!

The 1924 Olympic Games were the first to produce a number of competitors who were to become legendary. Besides Harold Abrahams

and Eric Liddell they produced Johnny 'Tarzan' Weissmuller who won three gold medals in swimming, and Helen Wills Moody who won the gold medal in women's tennis singles and went on to set a record of eight Wimbledon singles championships that stood until 1990 when Martina Navratilova won her ninth. Tennis was dropped from future Olympics before being restored in 1988. Benjamin Spock won a gold medal for rowing in the USA's winning eight and later became rather better known as a writer on childcare

*Dr Spock*

## CHARIOTS OF BRONZE

**Erik Vilen of Finland achieved the unique distinction of coming third in the 400 metres final and setting a new world record. The first**

*athlete home knocked down one of the hurdles and was for that reason denied the world record (though not, bizarrely, the gold medal); the second man was disqualified for straying from his lane, leaving Vilen to claim the record.*

The Finnish runner Paavo Nurmi wrote himself into Olympic history by winning five gold medals in distance events out of a total of 12 track medals he was to win over three Olympics – a record that is unlikely to be beaten. His habit of carrying a stopwatch while competing to check that he was pacing himself correctly had a disconcerting effect upon his competitors. The American swimmer Gertrude Ederle won a gold medal in the 400 metres relay team and two years later became the first woman to swim the English Channel. Her crossing time of 14 hours 30 minutes stood as a record for 24 years. In a foretaste of things to come Uruguay won the gold medal in football, repeating this feat in Amsterdam in 1928. This was the last time that rugby was played at the Olympics, leaving the victorious US team as the

reigning Olympic champions. The redoubtable Oscar Swahn was again selected for the Swedish shooting team at the age of 76 but was too unwell to compete, thus depriving himself of yet another record, having been competing in every Olympics since 1908. His son Alfred Swahn, however, did compete at Paris before retiring at a youthful 49 with three gold, three silver and three bronze medals. The 1924 Olympics were the first at which winter sports had their own separate competition. They were held at Chamonix and dominated by Scandinavian countries with Norway, Sweden and Finland winning nine of the 16 events. Germany, still in disgrace following the Great War, was not invited to the Paris Olympics though its allies Turkey, Austria and Hungary were allowed to compete.

## GOLDEN OLDIES

*Oscar Swahn was the oldest to compete in the Summer Olympics at the age of 72 years 280 days in 1920, having won a gold for shooting eight years earlier at a youthful 65 years 107 days. In 2006, at Turin, Anne Abernathy of the US Virgin Islands*

**became the oldest to enter the Winter Games at 52 years 10 months. Known as 'Grandma Luge', the Turin Games were her sixth Winter Olympics.**

**At Paris 44 nations were represented by 2,941 male and 131 female competitors.**

# Henri de Baillet-Latour (1876-1942)
*IOC President, 1925-42: the man who ticked off Hitler*

Count Henri de Baillet-Latour was rather surprisingly elected as President of the IOC when Pierre de Coubertin stepped down from the post in 1925. Baillet-Latour, a Belgian aristocrat and banker, was helped by the fact that he had taken on, with success, the task of organizing the Antwerp Olympics which took place in 1920 within two years of the ending of World War I. Having dealt with the aftermath of that war he then had to contend with the rise of the Nazi Party, the Berlin Games and the advent of World War II, challenges for which few would

have been equipped. His presidency could be portrayed as a sequence of reverses accompanied by appeasement though he has the unusual distinction of having reprimanded Hitler at the height of his power. First, however, he had to deal with the women. Like de Coubertin he was firmly opposed to the inclusion of women in the Olympics but his first retreat was executed on just that issue when they were admitted to five track and field events, though he staged a rally when, following the 'distress' of women competitors at the end of the 800 metres event in Amsterdam, he managed to have this excluded from the Olympics until 1960!

Baillet-Latour had supported the choice of Berlin for the Olympics of 1916 in the belief that the prospect of hosting the Games with Berlin on the world stage would discourage the notoriously vain Kaiser Wilhelm II from starting a war in the meantime. He seems to have pinned the same hopes on the German capital for 1936, de Coubertin also having approved of the choice, following which he was nominated by Germany for the Nobel Peace Prize. The prize went instead to a German opponent of the Nazis who died in Dachau concentration camp. As the Games approached Baillet-Latour became concerned about the treatment of Jewish athletes in Germany and wrote to three German members of the IOC to remind them that the Olympics had 'no political, racial, national or denominational character', leaving them the unenviable task of conveying this news to Hitler who toned down his rhetoric and actions against the Jews pending the advent of the Olympics, leaving in place the Jew Theodor Lewald who had secured the Games for Berlin and continued to serve as a German IOC representative until the Games were over. Having secured a further written guarantee concerning the participation of Jewish competitors in the Games, Baillet-Latour, in the words of the official history of the Olympics 'sank further into his state of appeasement'. He was one of those who promoted the expulsion from the IOC of the American Ernest Jahncke who had proposed a boycott of the Berlin Games.

However, he did show some

*Hitler*

backbone on the opening day of the Games when Hitler took it upon himself to congratulate publicly a number of German athletes who had won Germany's first ever gold medals in track and field, as well as congratulating three impeccably Aryan athletes from Finland. Baillet-Latour wrote to Hitler informing him that this was the prerogative of the

IOC at the medals ceremony and that if Hitler wished to congratulate medal winners he should do so in private. From that time Hitler conformed to the Belgian's instruction (possibly a unique event in history) though the incident became the basis of the legend that Hitler snubbed Jesse Owens by not congratulating him. In fact Owens did not compete until the next day by which time Hitler was behaving himself so the possibility of his publicly congratulating the

*Jesse Owens*

African-American did not arise. Baillet-Latour died in January 1942 shortly after hearing the news that his son, who was training with the Free Belgian air force in the USA, had been killed in an accident.

## Amsterdam 1928
*Eminent Victorians and distressed women*

At Amsterdam the stadium, for the first time, had a track whose circuit was 400 metres, a distance which would henceforth be the standard. The designer, Jan Wils, was appropriately the winner of the gold medal for architecture at the Amsterdam Games and for the first time the Olympic flame burned throughout the competition, having been lit on the Olympic tower not by an athlete but by an anonymous employee of the Amsterdam Electricity Company. As the Games began Baron de Coubertin addressed the competitors and referred to the supposed influence of two English clergymen: 'My thoughts turned to [Charles] Kingsley and [Thomas] Arnold and to the chapel at Rugby where the great clergyman rests who was, as I see it, one of the founders of athletic chivalry.' As we have seen, his attribution of enthusiasm for athletics to those two eminent Victorians, especially to Arnold, was undoubtedly mistaken but this error must be accorded a significant place in athletic history since the belief certainly influenced de Coubertin.

## HERE COME THE GIRLS

*At Amsterdam the proportion of female competitors was almost 10 per cent, more than double that achieved in Paris four years earlier. This was no accident. In 1922 a 'Women's Olympics' was held in Paris, inspired by a Frenchwoman called Alice Milliat (1884–1957) who was*

*Amsterdam 1928*

*determined to advance the cause of women in sport. When a second event was threatened in 1926 the IOC caved in and agreed to allow women to compete in five track and field events. Some IOC members thought this was the thin end of a wedge. Happily, they were right!*

For the first time women were allowed to compete in five track and field events but at the end of the 800 metres event the female competitors were adjudged to be in such a distressed state that the event was dropped from future Olympics and not restored until 1960, by which time, one assumes, the female form was thought to have toughened up.

## WOMEN'S EVENTS

*Women's distance running events were slow to establish themselves following the anxieties of Amsterdam. Having restored the 800 metres in 1960, the 1500 metres for women had to wait until Munich in 1972; in 1984 at Los Angeles the women's Marathon and 3,000 (later 5,000) metres followed but the 10,000 metres had to wait until 1988 at Seoul.*

Uruguay, as in 1924, won the football tournament, an achievement which encouraged that small South American country to stage the first World Cup two years later, thereby spawning the world's other great sporting competition. In the first World Cup Uruguay beat Argentina in the final – a foreboding event for the future of the game in which South America would come to have a dominant position. England's Football Association stood aloof from the competition until 1950 when England were duly humiliated by the USA.

## YOUNG, YOUNGER, YOUNGEST

*Reference has already been made to the possible participation of seven- or ten-year-old Marcel Depaille in the 1900 Paris Olympics, which may or may not be true. Dimitrios Loundras of Greece was recorded as being 10 years and 218 days when he came third in the gymnastic competition in 1896. There is little doubt about the age of Luigina Gavotti of Italy who took a silver in the team gymnastics for Italy in 1928 at 11 years and*

*302 days, while the British figure skater Cecilia Colledge was Britain's youngest Olympian at 11 years and 73 days in 1932. She became Britain's youngest medallist when she won silver for skating in 1936. The youngest swimming medal went to Inge Sorensen of Denmark who won bronze in breaststroke in 1936 at the age of 12 years 24 days. The youngest winners of gold medals were Marjorie Gestring of the USA in 1936 for diving at 13 years 267 days; the youngest male was Klaus Zerta who coxed the German pair to victory at Rome in 1960 at 13 years 283 days.*

Paavo Numri won his ninth and last gold medal in the 10,000 metres and a silver in the 3000 metres steeplechase in which event he was involved in a curious incident when he fell into the water jump during one of the qualifying heats, dropping the famous stopwatch that accompanied him in every race. The French runner Lucien Duquesne stopped and helped Nurmi to his feet. As the two runners approached the finishing line ahead of the rest of the field Nurmi invited Duquesne to break the tape ahead of him. The Frenchman courteously declined but his gesture was not rewarded by a medal in the final in which he came sixth. Some other personalities made themselves felt at Amsterdam. The manager of the US team was one Douglas MacArthur, later to achieve lasting fame as a general in the Pacific during World War II. King Olav V of Norway became the first reigning monarch to win a medal when he gained the gold in the sailing competition. Lord Burghley, having become, in 1927, the first person to complete the Trinity Great Court Run, now became the first member of the British House of Lords to win a gold medal, in the 400 metres hurdles. Later, as the Marquis of Exeter, he became vice-president of the IOC. He refused to allow his name to be used in *Chariots of Fire* because of the film's inaccurate depiction of historical events. The producers were no doubt consoled by the award of four Oscars, including that for best picture. Lord Andrew Lindsay, a fictional character, took his place but had many of Burghley's characteristics, including his habit

*Paavo Nurmi*

of practising hurdling by placing matchboxes (not champagne glasses as in the film) on each hurdle to test his ability to clear the hurdles cleanly. At Amsterdam 46 nations were represented by 2,611 male and 273 female competitors, the first time that women exceeded 10 per cent of the total competitors.

# Los Angeles 1932
*Cowboys and Coffee*

The Winter Olympics of 1932 were held at Lake Placid, New York State and were opened by the Governor of the State, Franklin D. Roosevelt, who was no doubt embarrassed by the fact that the unseasonally mild weather in February 1932 meant that snow had to be brought in by lorry from neighbouring Canada. Within a year Roosevelt would have replaced Herbert Hoover as President of the USA. Hoover became the first head of state not to attend a Summer Olympics in his country since he was too busy campaigning, unsuccessfully, for re-election as he was engulfed by the tragedy of the Great Depression. The Depression itself, together with the remoteness of California even to transatlantic liners, ensured that the number of competitors was less than half those which had been present at Amsterdam.

HOW MANY NATIONS?
*In the early Modern Olympics individuals entered on their own account rather than as representatives of their nations but even so only five nations have had their citizens present at every Modern Summer Olympics: Australia, France, Great Britain, Greece and Switzerland. France, Great Britain and Switzerland have also been represented at every Winter Games.*

The Los Angeles Memorial Coliseum, built in 1921 with a capacity of over 75,000 to commemorate the dead of World War I, was used for the first, but not the last, time for Olympic athletic events. Six months before the games were due to start not a single nation had entered a team but a strong publicity drive by the city

*Los Angeles 1932*

of Los Angeles, accompanied by a promise that the opening ceremony would be attended by Douglas Fairbanks, Mary Pickford and Charlie Chaplin, ensured that 37 national teams arrived for the event and the opening was attended by a record number of spectators who filled the stadium. It was also used for the Los Angeles Games of 1984, becoming the only facility to be used for two separate Olympic Games. The famous Pasadena Rose Bowl was used for cycling. For the first time an Olympic Village was purpose-built for male athletes in the Baldwin Hills outside the city, providing work for some of California's unemployed, but although the facilities were very comfortable they had some drawbacks. Female athletes were accommodated in a Los Angeles hotel while the village was fiercely guarded by cowboys who, in that more puritanical age, enforced a strict segregation of the sexes, even excluding the Finland team's female cook from their quarters. The Finns were also missing Paavo Nurmi. At the age of 35 he had intended to contest the 10,000 metres and Marathon but was excluded because

the Swedish athletic federation, headed by the future IOC President Sigrid Edstrom, argued that he had compromised his amateur status by accepting excessive expenses for a tour of Germany. The Finns objected to the ban but were overruled, leading to a boycott by Finns of athletics events in Sweden for many years. The French were happier since, despite the imposition of Prohibition in the USA (it was abolished the following year), the French team was

*Charlie Chaplin*

*Cowboy guardian of public morality*

allowed to import the wine without which they couldn't live and which was to be a bone of contention at the London Olympics of 1948 (see below). The team from Brazil was the unhappiest of all. The impoverished Brazilian athletics authorities, beset by the Great Depression, despatched the team to Los Angeles on a warship equipped with a large consignment of coffee which the team were supposed

to sell to cover their expenses. Frustrated by import controls which forbade them to land the coffee, only 24 of the team could afford the $1 landing fee.

## FINLAND REJOICE

*The Finns were delighted when the Swedish silver medallist in the equestrian event, Bertil Sandstrom, was deprived of his medal and demoted to last for 'clicking' his horse in encouragement. His protestation that the noise was made by a creaking saddle were unavailing but for the Finns it was a modest revenge for their loss of Paavo Nurmi at the behest of Sweden.*

There were two innovations at the Los Angeles Olympics which have remained a feature of later games. The first was the use of the 'Kirby two-eyed camera' for photo-finishes. The invention, by Gustavus Kirby of Columbia University, focussed one 'eye' on the finish line and the other on a chronometer recording the time. It was used to determine the result of the 100 metres where, to the naked eye, two runners called Tolan and Metcalfe appeared to cross the finish line together but the camera showed that Tolan's torso crossed the line first. He gained the gold medal. The second innovation concerned the victory ceremony where, for the first time, a three-tiered stand was used and national flags were raised as medals were presented. Every athletic record was broken at Los Angeles except the long jump which had to wait four more years for Jesse Owens. In the 3000 metres steeplechase an extra lap was run owing to the inattention of an absent-minded official, though the result of the event was not thought to have been affected. The first gender-related issue occurred, unnoticed, in the Los Angeles Games when Poland's Stanislawa Walasiewicz won the gold medal in the women's 100 metres, following this with the silver medal in the event four years later. After her death in 1980, it was discovered that she was transgender and would have been ineligible to participate in later contests.

Baron Nishi won Japan's first (and so far only) gold medal for equestrian events in show jumping and later died in World War II in the defence of the Japanese island of Iwo Jima, being represented in Clint Eastwood's film *Letters from Iwo Jima*. But the undoubted star of the games was the American female athlete 'Babe' Didrikson. Five women's athletic events were included, each woman being allowed to enter a maximum of three events, and Babe Didrikson, 'The Dallas Cyclone' – having announced 'I came out here to beat everybody in sight' – duly won gold medals in the 80 metre hurdles and the javelin. In the high jump she had to settle for silver despite clearing the same height as the gold medallist with the same number of jumps. The judges, baffled, ruled that her jumping style was illegal, her head having crossed the bar before her body (a technique now universally adopted at international level). She remains the only athlete to have won medals for running, jumping and throwing. She later married a wrestler called George Zaharias and, as 'Babe Zaharias', took up golf after leaving athletics, becoming a champion golfer and winning the British and American Ladies' amateur titles. At Los Angeles

'Olympic Merit' awards were given to two Germans, not for competing successfully at the games but for being the first people to scale the North Face of the Matterhorn.

## HOW MANY EVENTS?

*As the numbers of separate sports in the Olympics has inexorably increased with the addition of activities like tennis, rugby and synchronized swimming, it is helpful to reflect that only five sports have been present at every Modern Olympics: athletics, swimming, cycling, gymnastics and fencing. The Beijing Olympics of 2008 featured 302 events in 28 sports, an 'event' being an individual competition within a sport, e.g. the 100 metres is an event within athletics.*

*At Los Angeles 37 nations were represented by 1,209 male and 124 female competitors.*

# Berlin, 1936
*Hitler and the 'Black Auxiliaries'*

The 1936 Olympics are undoubtedly the most notorious to date because of the involvement of Hitler and the Nazis though the Games were awarded to Berlin in 1931, two years before Hitler came to power in Germany. And there was disagreement in the Nazi hierarchy about whether the event should go ahead at all. Heinrich Himmler, head of the SS, opposed the idea and at an early meeting Hitler declared that the Olympics were 'an invention of Jews and Freemasons' which 'could not be tolerated in a Reich ruled by the National Socialists'. But Hitler was persuaded by Josef Goebbels that

*Berlin 1936*

the Olympics would enable him to practise to an unprecedented degree the black arts of propaganda at which he excelled. Hitler saw the link with the Ancient Games as the perfect way to illustrate his belief that Classical Greece was an Aryan forerunner of the modern German Reich. In March 1936, as the Olympics approached, German troops marched into the Rhineland in clear violation of the Treaty of Versailles. There were protests and talk of boycotting the Olympics but no action was taken.

## A SPANISH BOYCOTT

*The left-wing Popular Front government of Spain boycotted the Berlin Olympics and organized the 'People's Olympiad' in Barcelona. Six thousand athletes from 22 countries registered, but the games were aborted because of the outbreak of the Spanish Civil War which occurred just as the event was due to start. Spain, along with the Soviet Union, did not take part in the 1936 Summer Olympics.*

Hitler's favourite architect Albert Speer, who later wrote an arresting account of his life as a top Nazi entitled *Inside the Third Reich*, put the finishing touches to the Olympic stadium and for the first time the Olympic flame, kindled as previously at Olympia, was borne to Berlin by a relay of 3,331 torchbearers who covered 1,980 miles in twelve days. Its passage through Vienna sparked a pro-Nazi demonstration following the Anschluss which had seen Austria annexed to the German Reich. The Krupp armaments company produced the torches in wood and metal, designed to look like an olive leaf. Is the Olympic torch relay the only remaining legacy of the Third Reich? At the opening ceremony the spectators heard music specially composed for the occasion by the celebrated composer Richard Strauss and as Hitler observed the opening ceremony the teams marched past, some giving the Nazi salute with the raised right arm while others, notably the British and Americans, confined themselves to 'eyes right'. In an ironic twist Spiridon Louis, who had won the first modern Marathon at the Athens Olympics 40 years earlier, then presented the German dictator with an olive branch from Olympia as a symbol of the 'Olympic Peace'. A further innovation, the work of Goebbels, was the provision of broadcasting facilities of unprecedented quality in what may be called the first 'media city'. Twenty transmission vans were provided for journalists and events were broadcast in 28 languages. For the first time television beamed pictures to a number of halls in the Berlin area.

Before the athletes and spectators arrived in Berlin, posters hostile to Jews and other groups were removed and a German-born Jew called Helene Mayer, who had emigrated with her family to America to escape persecution, was persuaded to return for the Games and compete for Nazi Germany in the fencing competition, having been declared a kind of honorary Aryan. She won the silver medal in the foil, the gold and bronze medals also being won by Jews. She was criticized by the American Jewish community for representing Germany, which she always thought of as her country, and further criticized when she gave the Nazi salute on the podium at the

medal ceremony, insisting that she did so to protect those members of her family who remained in Germany. After the defeat of the Nazi regime in World War II she returned to live in Germany where she died in 1953.

## TROUBLES WITH JEWS

*Hitler was furious when he learned that Theodor Lewald, the patriotic German who had secured the Olympics for Berlin, had a Jewish grandmother. Hitler demanded that Lewald be removed from the organizing committee but his knowledge and contacts were indispensable so it was agreed that he would resign as Germany's IOC representative when the Games finished. The Fuehrer was even angrier when he discovered that Captain Wolfgang Fuerstner, the extremely efficient officer who ran the male athletes' village so well, also had a Jewish ancestor. Fuerstner was fired. The women were separately accommodated near the stadium on the grounds that 'after long and intense training women are very highly strung immediately before difficult contests'.*

However, there were some happier moments. At the Berlin Olympics basketball was introduced to the Games, the first game being started by a 75-year-old Canadian clergyman called James Naismith who had invented the sport the previous century as a means of encouraging people to take exercise, indoors, during the cold winters in Massachusetts where he worked as a PE instructor. The American Glenn Morris, having won the decathlon, received his medal from Hitler's mistress Eva Braun and conducted a brief affair with Hitler's favourite film maker Leni Riefenstahl. He followed in Johnny Weissmuller's jungle footsteps to play Tarzan. Leni Riefenstahl later made a film of the Berlin Games, *Olympia*, in which she re-staged part of the torch relay.

The greatest controversy over the Olympics, of course, concerned the achievements of the black American athlete James Cleveland (JC or 'Jesse') Owens, dismissed by the Nazi press as one of the 'black auxiliaries' in the US team. Owens won four gold medals of the seven gold, three silver and three bronze medals won by America's black competitors. It is usually forgotten that the black Americans were loudly cheered by the German crowds who do not appear to have shared the racist views of their obnoxious leaders. And few have commented on the helpful advice given to Jesse Owens by his German rival Luz Long in the long jump. Owens' first two jumps were declared void because he overran the take-off board so Long suggested that he start his run-up from a little further back. Owens' third and final jump of 8.06 metres won the gold medal and set a record that remained until 1960, leaving the gallant Long with the silver. Afterwards the two men walked arm in arm from the field. Long and Owens remained friends and corresponded regularly until the war began in which Long was killed during the Allied invasion of Sicily. After the war Jesse Owens remained in touch with Long's son until Owens died in 1980. There was one final twist in the story of Jesse Owens. The American team manager, Avery Brundage (later a long-serving and controversial IOC President), anxious to win the 4 × 100 metres relay, decided to include Owens and another black medal winner, Ralph Metcalfe, in place of Mart Glickman and Sam Stoller. The Americans won, Owens took his fourth gold medal and Glickman and Stoller lost out. They were both Jews but the change was probably due to the American team's evaluation of its prospects, not to racism.

## SO WHO'S BEING RACIST?

*Hearing it suggested that Hitler had snubbed him for racist reasons by not publicly congratulating him, Jesse Owens recalled that as a black athlete he was obliged to live separately from white compatriots during events in the USA and commented, 'I wasn't invited up to shake hands with Hitler. But I wasn't invited to the White House to shake hands with the President either.' During the Olympics Adi Dassler persuaded Jesse Owens to use Adidas running shoes with their distinctive three-stripe logo, the first such 'sponsorship' deal with a black athlete.*

*At Berlin 49 nations were represented by 3,606 males and 330 females.*

## SIGRID EDSTROM, IOC PRESIDENT, 1946-52

Following the death of Henri de Baillet-Latour during the war, the Swede Sigrid Edstrom (1870-1964) was elected as fourth President of the IOC. Sigrid held the office for only six years, second only in brevity to the first President Vikelas in an institution which has traditionally attracted those who clung to office. He is chiefly remembered for overseeing the award of the first post-war Olympics to London and, less gloriously, for leading the Swedish objection to the participation of the Finnish national hero, Paavo Nurmi, in the Los Angeles Olympics of 1932 on the grounds that expenses paid to Nurmi during a tour of Germany had compromised his amateur status, a move that caused difficulties between the two nations for many years.

# RECOVERING FROM ANOTHER WAR

## London 1948: The Austerity Olympics
*Craven A and 'Looking into Underpants'*

The 1948 Olympics, like those of 1908, came to London at short notice. Continental Europe was devastated and so London, bombed out and beset by rationing, offered its services just as it had done when Rome pulled out 40 years earlier. The Prime Minister, Clement Attlee, believed that the Olympic Games would draw much-needed foreign currency into Britain's beleaguered economy. At a time when even bread was rationed (as it had not been during the war itself) British competitors received extra food rations but the main advantage of being chosen for the British team, at a time when an adult could buy one shirt or blouse every 20 months, was a free uniform: jacket, trousers or skirt, tie, hat and plimsolls (trainers

had not yet been invented), all 'off ration'. Unable to buy suitable shorts off ration, one of the oarsmen at Henley wore a pair fashioned by his mother from an old towel. With two weeks to go fewer than half the available tickets had been sold but once the competitions began and were reported on wireless and in the press, public interest grew and a black market in tickets developed. Athletes were accommodated in disused RAF camps and in schools during the summer holidays and Boy Scouts with bicycles were encouraged to make themselves available on these premises to act as messengers, the incentive being a free lunch. One member of the French team who was caught selling black market tickets explained that he had no choice. His foreign currency allowance of £9 had been inadequate so he had invested some of it in two shilling (10 pence) tickets and was now selling them at a handsome profit to make ends meet! The French report on the games devoted 12 of its 14 pages to complaints about inadequate food and the difficulties in securing duty-free entry for their supplies of finest Mouton-Rothschild claret. Other signs of the times were the construction of Wembley's Olympic Way by German prisoners of war and the sponsorship of the games by Craven A cigarettes! Neither Germany nor Japan was invited to the Games on the grounds that neither had a government in place with which to negotiate. The Soviet Union chose not to attend though representatives of the Soviet Embassy attended every event and informed Stalin that the Games were an opportunity to exhibit the superiority of socialism.

## WILSON AND LAURIE

*One of the greatest comebacks in sporting history was that of Jack Wilson and Ran Laurie at the 1948 Games in the coxless pairs at Henley. Multiple Cambridge Blues of the 1930s, they won the event at Henley in 1938 and spent the war years in the Sudan. In 1948 they both returned to London on leave and at the age of 33 resumed rowing 'for fun' after a gap of ten years. In the absence of other British competitors they entered the Olympic coxless*

*pairs on behalf of Great Britain and won at a canter. The actor Hugh Laurie, also a Cambridge rowing Blue, is Ran Laurie's son.*

Names now familiar to us appeared in unusual circumstances. As the opening ceremony began, the British team, who would enter the Wembley stadium last, realized that they had no flag. A young medical student, who was acting as assistant to Harold 'Chariots of Fire' Abrahams (treasurer of the organizing committee), was despatched to retrieve one from a distant car. Fortunately he could run fast. His name was Roger Bannister and within six years he would run the first sub-four-minute mile. The manager of the British amateur football team was one Matt Busby who, in accordance with the wishes of the sponsors, handed out Craven A cigarettes at his team talk! The team reached the semi-final where they were knocked out by the flagrantly professional Yugoslav side, thus heralding disputes over amateurism and professionalism which rumbled on until the 1980s when the professionals won. Kenneth 'they think it's all over' Wolstenholme made his debut as a football commentator but perhaps Britain's greatest hero was, Jim Halliday who won a bronze medal in weightlifting despite having emerged from a spell as a prisoner of the Japanese war weighing four stone. Emil Zatopek, the Hungarian soldier whose loping style of running looked so painful, lapped all the other

*Emil Zatopek*

competitors in the 10,000 metres, a foretaste of his achievements at Helsinki, and it was he who declared that the London Games were 'the sun finally coming out after the war'. The games cost £732,268 (the estimate for 2012 is over £9 billion) and yielded a profit of £29,420 as well as injecting some foreign currencies into Britain's strained economy. If the Games of 2012 do as well, then many will be surprised and all will be pleased.

The 1948 Games can boast one 'first' and two 'lasts'. The first was gender-checking which involved doctors 'looking into the underpants of competitors to check for sexual abnormalities'. One hopes that Fanny Blankers-Koen, the great Dutch woman who won four gold medals for her astonishing sprinting, was exempted from this process, given that she had borne two children.

## THE FLYING DUTCHWOMAN

*Francina 'Fanny' Blankers-Koen had set world records in the long jump, high jump, sprint and hurdling events before World War II, and continued to break records during that conflict despite the severe shortage of food which she suffered along with her fellow citizens. At the 1948 London Olympics, 30 years old and already a mother of two, she won gold medals in the 100 metres, 200 metres, 80 metres hurdles and the 4 × 100 metres relay, more than any other competitor. The 80 metres hurdles had such a close finish that it was some time before the judges could decide, from photographs, whether Fanny had beaten the Briton Maureen Gardner to the tape. A moment of panic ensued for Dutch spectators when the band struck up 'God Save the King' but relief followed when it became clear that it was greeting the arrival of King George VI. No-one has ever beaten this tally in athletics though some, including Jesse Owens, have matched it. But he wasn't pregnant at the time, as Fanny was with her third child!*

The first 'last' was the award of medals for art, architecture, literature, painting and music following a competition held at the Victoria and Albert Museum. The reason for

their abandonment was that it was considered that entrants were in practice professionals. The second last was the ten kilometre walk which was won by the Swede Ingemar Johansson, not to be confused with his boxing namesake whose feats dazzled the 1952 Olympics. The ten kilometre walk joined many events which flourished briefly in the Olympics before being discarded. One feature of the London Games that was little remarked at the time was the competition for veterans of World War II with spinal injuries. This took place at Stoke Mandeville Hospital in Buckinghamshire which was beginning to develop expertise in treating such injuries and was the beginning of the flourishing Paralympic movement.

## TWO-HANDED THROWING AND ALL THAT

*Discontinued events include the following, the year in brackets indicating the last year in which the event was included in the Olympics: 60 metres sprint (1904); cross-country (1924); standing high and long jumps*

*(1912) and triple jump (1904); two-handed discus, shot and javelin (using each hand in turn, the aggregate distance counting for the result, all 1912); rope-climbing (1932); club swinging (1932); tumbling (1932); live-pigeon shooting (1900); cricket (1900); coxed 16-man naval rowing (1906); roque (an American version of croquet, 1904).*

*At the London Games 59 nations were represented by 3,702 male and 390 female competitors.*

## Avery Brundage
*IOC President 1952-72*

*Avery Brundage*

In 1952 Avery Brundage (1887–1985) was elected fifth President of the IOC, the only US citizen to hold the office. He was born in Detroit and competed in the Stockholm Olympics of 1912 where he finished 6th in the pentathlon and 16th in the decathlon, both events being won by his compatriot Jim Thorpe. Brundage appears to have felt little affection for Thorpe following the latter's disqualification and had a hand in drawing attention to Thorpe's participation in professional baseball. It was not until ten years after Brundage's retirement from the presidency of the IOC that Thorpe was forgiven and his medals returned to his family, Thorpe himself having been dead for almost 20 years. Brundage's career as an administrator was rarely short of controversy, both as IOC President and, previously, as President of the United States Olympic Committee. In 1936 he opposed the boycotting of the Berlin

Olympics despite the anti-semitic policies of Hitler and he became a member of the IOC in that year only as a result of the expulsion of his fellow American Ernest Lee Jahncke.

## ERNEST LEE JAHNCKE (1877-1960)

*In a letter to IOC president Henri de Baillet-Latour, Jahncke, of German descent, had written: 'Neither Americans nor the representatives of other countries can take part in the Games in Nazi Germany without at least acquiescing in the contempt of the Nazis for fair play and their sordid exploitation of the Games.' For this he became the first person to be expelled from the IOC by a vote of its members. He was the only person to emerge from the affair with credit and was replaced by Brundage.*

Brundage branded the proposed boycott of the Berlin Games 'a Jewish-Communist conspiracy' and it has been suggested that the late decision to replace two Jews in the United States relay team, Glickman and Stoller, with the black Jesse Owens and Ralph Metcalfe was

influenced by Brundage's belief that Hitler would be less offended by black victors than Jewish ones, though Owens and Metcalfe were certainly worth their places. He raised no objection to the widespread use of the Nazi salute at the Berlin Games but had Tommie Smith and John Carlos expelled from the Olympic Village in Mexico in 1968 for giving the Black Power salute on the victory rostrum. After the Olympics Brundage's construction company was awarded the contract to build the German embassy in Washington. He could not be described as progressive in other ways either. He opposed the participation of women in athletic events, declaring, 'I am fed up to the ears with women as track and field competitors.' In 1972 at Munich he took the brave decision, controversial at the time but later adjudged correct, to continue the Games after the massacre of Israeli athletes. In 1972 he at last resigned as IOC President in protest at the decision to exclude Rhodesia from the Olympics, a decision taken because of the racist policies of Ian Smith's rebel white minority regime. Brundage declared,

'Much of the world had judged until now that the IOC was the only international organization capable of resisting opportunism and political blackmail and now it has committed suicide.'

Brundage was a fierce protector of the amateur ethos of the Olympics and believed that this would promote international harmony. His opening address as IOC President was a sermon on amateurism. He declared that, 'The moral and spiritual values of fair play based on honesty, justice, impartiality and dignity are essential for a better world. If they are developed on the friendly field of sport they will undoubtedly be adopted in other areas.' He had the Austrian skier Karl Schranz expelled from the 1972 Winter Games for accepting sponsorship but his commitment to amateurism was tinged with pragmatism which amounted to hypocrisy. When it was observed that Soviet bloc athletes were, to all intents and purposes, professionals he dismissed the claim by saying it was 'their way of life': true, but missing the point. His resignation as president the same

year was unmourned. Following his 20-year reign the IOC rules were amended so that the president now holds office for eight years, renewable for a further four years.

## A COLOURFUL PRIVATE LIFE

*Brundage's private life was not without interest. In 1927 he had married but in 1951-2 he had two sons by his Finnish mistress, his name being omitted from their birth certificates to avoid scandal, as at the time he was moving towards the presidency of the IOC. Two years before his death, at the age of 85, he married a 36-year-old German called Marianne Reuss.*

# Helsinki 1952
## *The Hungarians arrive*

Helsinki, with its population of 367,000, was the smallest city ever to host the Summer Olympic Games. The opening ceremony was disturbed when a mentally confused young woman, clad in a flowing white robe and proclaiming herself to be the

'Angel of Peace', ran around the track to the bewilderment of the crowd. This was soon forgotten, however, when the great Finnish athlete Paavo Nurmi was seen to be entering the stadium bearing the Olympic torch. At the Winter Olympics in Oslo the previous February the opening ceremony was a subdued event since the small British team was seen to be wearing black armbands to mark the fact that it was also the day of the funeral of King George VI. The Helsinki Olympics were the first at which the Soviet Union, Israel and Communist China were represented. As so often, the United States headed the medals table, followed by the Soviet Union. For the first time the Olympics became a proxy for the Cold War between those superpowers, the medals tally being seen as evidence of the superiority of one political system over another. At this time, of course, the Olympics were strictly amateur but the USA, with its 'sports scholarships' at American universities, enabled its young athletes to train without the inconvenience of having to work for a living. At the same time an amazing proportion of Soviet athletes were found posts in the Soviet armed forces without having to spend too much time on sentry duty. The paranoia of the Soviet delegation, still under the rule of Stalin, was shown by their insistence that their athletes stay in a village separate from the other competitors, presumably fearing infection from the capitalists they would encounter there.

However, the most extraordinary achievement was undoubtedly that of the Hungarian team. Despite having

*Helsinki 1952*

a population of barely 9 million (not much more than the population of London at the time) their team came third in the medals table with 42 medals, including 16 golds. One of these was in the football tournament, won by Hungary's 'golden team' led by Ferenc Puskas which, the following year, was to inflict upon England their first ever defeat at Wembley by an overseas side, winning by 6 goals to 3 and setting a pattern for the future. However, the most astonishing individual achievement was by the team's 10,000 metres gold medallist from London, Emil Zatopek, whose agonising, loping running style carried him to three gold medals. Having won the 5,000 and 10,000 metres event Zatopek decided to enter the Marathon. Running the distance for the first time, he wasn't sure how fast he should run. After 19 kilometres, baffled by the slow pace, he enquired of the leading runner, Jim Peters of Great Britain, 'Can't you go any faster?' Peters couldn't but Zatopek could and won the event by 750 yards, beating the previous Olympic record for the event by six minutes. His wife Dana, with whom

he shared a birthday, added to the team and family tally by winning the gold medal in the javelin.

Two boxers stepped on to the world stage for the first time, though in very different circumstances. The future world heavyweight champion Floyd Patterson, from the USA, won the middleweight gold medal and turned professional. The Swede Ingemar Johansson was disqualified in the

*Ference Puskas*

heavyweight division for 'not trying'. In 1959, in a sensational bout in New York, Johansson knocked out Floyd Patterson to become the first world heavyweight champion born outside the USA. Britain had to wait until almost the last day of the Helsinki Games for its first gold medal, won by Sir Harry Llewellyn on Foxhunter in show jumping.

### THE PARALYMPICS ARE BORN

*Ludwig Guttmann (1899–1980) was born in Germany to an orthodox Jewish family and trained as a neurologist, leaving Germany for England in the face of persecution in 1939. He set up the spinal injuries unit at Stoke Mandeville hospital in 1944 and, believing that sport was therapeutic, organized the Stoke Mandeville Games for British World War II veterans in 1948. In 1952 they were joined by injured Dutch veterans and the Paralympic movement was born, achieving full recognition at Rome in 1960. Guttmann is now recognized as one of the true heroes of the Olympic movement.*

*At Helsinki 69 nations were represented by 4,922 male and 507 female competitors.*

# Melbourne 1956
## *'Boxing Under Water'*

The Melbourne Olympics of 1956 were the first to be held in the southern hemisphere though an exception was made for the equestrian competitions. Strict Australian quarantine regulations led to the equestrian events being held in Stockholm while the Winter Olympics were held in Cortina d'Ampezzo, Italy, the cost being met by a levy on Italian football pools. As at Lake Placid, New York, in 1932, snow had to be imported from various locations before the competition could begin. Many had doubts about the wisdom of holding the 'Summer' Games in Australia during the northern winter and this wasn't helped by what was perceived as the half-hearted approach of the Australian authorities who, faced with a housing shortage, were unwilling to spend much on an Olympic village.

Avery Brundage, the American who was President of the IOC, estimated that Rome, which was scheduled to host the games in 1960, was better prepared and asked the Italian authorities to be ready to take the place of Melbourne. This appears to have galvanized the Australian Federal and State governments and the Melbourne Olympics duly began on 22nd November, during the Australian summer, and took place in the shadow of unsettling political turmoil which influenced the Games themselves.

The invasion of Egypt by Britain, France and Israel in an attempt to wrest control of the Suez Canal from the Egyptian regime of Colonel Nasser, had infuriated the United States and offended much of the rest of the world including the Soviet Union. Very soon afterwards the Soviet Union took advantage of the discomfiture of the Western allies to invade Hungary and suppress an uprising against the Communist regime which had been imposed upon Hungary by the Russians. The Melbourne Olympics were thus the first to suffer significantly from

boycotts though these would be a feature of future games. Iraq, the Lebanon and Egypt withdrew over Suez; the Netherlands, Spain and neutral Switzerland over Hungary; and Communist China boycotted the games in protest at an entry from Formosa, as Taiwan was then called, the former government of China. The climax to this ill-feeling occurred in a water-polo match between Hungary and the Soviet Union which was abandoned by the Swedish referee since, in his words, it had become 'a boxing match under water'. The match was referred to in the press as 'The Blood in the Water Match'. John Kelly Jr, son of Jack and brother of Princess Grace of Monaco, added to the family's collection of medals with a bronze in the sculls.

The Melbourne Olympics revealed to the world the astonishing talents of the Ukrainian soldier Vladimir Kuts. His position in the Soviet military meant that he was, for practical purposes, a professional athlete though according to the Communist regime professional sportsmen did not exist within its system. However, nothing could detract from the fact

*Vladimir Kuts*

Helsinki after striking a barrier. In the meantime Brasher, a Cambridge graduate employed by an oil company, had helped Roger Bannister run a mile in less than four minutes but for Melbourne he was Britain's second-string runner to John Disley who was one of the favourites for the event. Running with his trademark spectacles held on with Elastoplast, Brasher won the event but was promptly disqualified for supposedly impeding a Norwegian runner called Larson. Neither Larson nor the other athletes involved supported the disqualification, which was revoked. Would athletes behave today as Larson did in 1956? A new and pleasing innovation of the Melbourne Games was proposed to the IOC in a

that Kuts not only won the 5,000 and 10,000 metres events but did so by humiliating margins at the expense of Britain's Gordon Pirie. He repeatedly broke world records for the two distances. Rumours that he was given drugs to enhance his performance were never substantiated though in later life he became very overweight and died in 1975 aged only 48. Britain won its first track medal since 1932 in the unexpected form of Chris Brasher who had come 11th out of 12 athletes in the final of the 3,000 metres steeplechase in

*Chris Brasher*

letter from an Australian schoolboy of Chinese extraction called John Wing. He suggested that for the closing ceremony all the athletes should enter the stadium together, a practice first adopted at Melbourne and continued in subsequent Olympics.

---

## MILES AND MARATHONS

*Chris Brasher and Christopher Chataway had acted as pacemakers for Roger Bannister when he broke the four-minute barrier for the mile on 6 May 1954, when Bannister covered the distance in 3 minutes 59.4 seconds on the track at Iffley Road, Oxford. Brasher acted as pacemaker for two laps and Chris Chataway for the third. Harold Abrahams disapproved of the 'professionalism' that he discerned in the pacemaking. Chataway later became a Member of Parliament and Brasher instituted the London Marathon.*

*At Melbourne 67 nations were represented by 3,184 male and 363 female competitors; to these must be added 147 male and 12 female competitors at equestrian events in Stockholm.*

---

# Rome 1960
*Ethiopians and steamy bathrooms*

The Winter Olympics of 1960 took place in Squaw Valley, California where the opening ceremony was directed by Walt Disney and attended by Richard Nixon, Vice-President of the United States, soon to be defeated by John F. Kennedy for the presidency before gaining it for himself in 1968. South Africa competed in the Summer Olympics for the last time until 1992, the intervening years being overshadowed by the issue of apartheid and the numerous boycotts associated with it. Taiwan, formerly Formosa, competed for the first time. There were some others 'firsts' as well, not all good. Knut Jensen, a Danish cyclist, died as a result of taking performance-enhancing drugs. On a happier note, for the first time the Marathon ended not in the Olympic stadium but at the Arch of Constantine. It was run in the evening to avoid the heat of the day and the last few kilometres were run past the catacombs of the historic Appian Way which was spectacularly lit for the runners by soldiers bearing torches. Moreover, the event was won by the first of a continuing line of African long-distance runners whose upbringing at high altitudes prepared them for the event. Abebe Bikila was a private soldier in the Imperial bodyguard of Emperor Haile Selassie of Ethiopia. Bikila had been born in 1935, the year Mussolini launched the invasion of Ethiopia. Reports of the unknown African's prowess as a runner had been dismissed in well-informed circles as fantasy. A report that he had run a Marathon faster than the great Zatopek was put down to Africans' inability to measure the distance correctly. So the crowd was amazed when he reached the finish not only some distance ahead of the field but in a time of two hours, fifteen minutes eight seconds, a full eight minutes faster than Zatopek, before entertaining the crowd with his callisthenic 'warming down' exercises. In Tokyo, four years later, he won in another record time, five weeks after having had his appendix removed, and in the following Olympics in Mexico City the Marathon was won by another Ethiopian, Mamo Wolde. Following a car accident in 1969 which injured his legs Bikila took up archery.

Britain won two gold medals in Rome, each of them a result of astonishing dedication. The first was that of Anita Lonsborough in the 200 metres breaststroke. Anita was noted for her relaxed attitude at the start of races and was seen to be manicuring her nails shortly before the start of the Olympic final while wondering whether she would swallow a fly buzzing above the water into which she was about to dive. She was also a stoic, accepting without complaint the decision of her employers,

*Anita Lonsbrough*

Huddersfield Corporation, to dock her wages for the time she spent training during her lunch hour! She was the only winner of a swimming event who was not from the USA or Australia. Even more amazing, perhaps, was the dedication of Don Thompson, the five feet five inches tall insurance clerk from Hillingdon who took up race walking in 1951 at the age of 18 and followed his victory in the 1955 London to Brighton walk with seven further successes in the same event. At the Melbourne Games he had collapsed when approaching the stadium but his preparations for Rome left nothing to chance. Besides outdoor training at 4 am to avoid arriving late for work he exercised on a treadmill in his bathroom using heaters and steam kettles to simulate the conditions he expected in Rome. This paid off. He was prepared for the 38 degrees centigrade heat in which the 50 km race was held in Rome and he won the gold medal in a new Olympic record time of four hours 25 minutes 30 seconds, easily defeating all the post-war Olympic walking champions in the process. The Italians affectionately named him 'Il Topolino'

('The Little Mouse').

The Rome Olympics also saw the arrival of some other remarkable athletes. An 18-year-old American called Cassius Clay won the light-heavyweight boxing competition, many onlookers commenting on his remarkable speed of foot and fist for such a big man. Within four years he became world professional heavyweight champion before changing his name to 'Muhammad Ali'. The games also saw the arrival on the scene of the Ukrainian sisters Irina and Tamara Press who won gold medals for the Soviet team in 80 metres hurdles and pentathlon (Irina) and shot put and discus (Tamara), also winning medals at the Tokyo Games four years later. Their careers ended when effective gender checking was introduced after the Tokyo Games. No such doubts surrounded King Constantine of Greece who, in the sailing competition, became the second reigning monarch to win a gold medal, following that of King Olav of Norway in 1928. At Rome, for the first time, a separate event was held for disabled athletes who were not necessarily war veterans, another step along the path towards a fully fledged Paralympic movement. These were known at the time as the 9th Annual International Stoke Mandeville Games though they are now recognized as the first Paralympic Games.

At Rome 83 nations were represented by 4,717 male and 596 female competitors.

## Tokyo 1964
*Cold, wet and waterlogged – fortunately for Britain*

The Winter Olympics were held at Innsbruck in Austria and were dogged by the shortage of snow which was now almost becoming an Olympic tradition. On this occasion the Austrian army came to the rescue, bringing lorry-loads of snow from cooler areas of the Alps. The Olympic flame at the opening ceremony of the Summer Olympics (the first ever held in Asia) was lit by a young runner who had been born in the vicinity of Hiroshima on 6 August 1945, the day that the city was devastated by the world's first attack by atomic weapons. East and West Germany

competed as one nation for the last time until the two parts of Germany were reunited for the 1992 Barcelona Games, compromising on Beethoven's setting of Schiller's 'Ode to Joy' from his 9th symphony as their joint anthem. The Tokyo Games witnessed remarkable achievements by two Commonwealth athletes: Peter Snell of New Zealand and the rebellious Australian swimmer Dawn Fraser. Dawn Fraser had been suspended from competition when only 14 years old in 1951 for 'professionalism' on the grounds that she had competed for trophies – though there was a suspicion that this was a rap across the knuckles for a schoolgirl who was not sufficiently deferential

*Dawn Fraser and team-mate Ilsa Konrads*

towards authority figures and who regularly beat male swimmers. The suspension was soon revoked and she won gold medals at Melbourne and Rome before being banned from the opening ceremony in Tokyo for indiscipline (she sneaked in anyway with the complicity of sympathetic team-mates) and winning another gold in the 100 metres freestyle and silver in the 100 metres relay. In the meantime Dawn had fallen out with the management of the Australian team for refusing to swim the butterfly leg in a medley relay but her final offence involved removing a flag from the Imperial Palace in Tokyo which triggered a diplomatic incident. For this escapade she was suspended from swimming for ten years but since she had reached the age of 27 by the time of the Tokyo Olympics, near the upper limit for a swimmer, her career was effectively over anyway. Peter Snell became the first athlete to win both the 800 and 1500 metres since the Briton Albert Hill at the Antwerp Games of 1920.

Britain won four gold medals at Tokyo, two of them in the long jump events and neither of them

*Lynn Davies*

anticipated. In unseasonably cold, wet and windy weather the Welshman Lynn Davies defeated the American favourite Ralph Boston while Mary Rand won the women's event in similar conditions. The weather and the water-logged run-up favoured the British competitors whose coach, Ron Pickering, had instituted a training regime emphasizing the development of strong thigh muscles which coped well with such conditions. Ann Packer, who later married the captain of the British team Robbie Brightwell, won the

800 metres event which she had not intended to enter since she considered herself to be a sprinter. She had planned to go shopping on the afternoon concerned but, learning that her fiancé had narrowly failed to win a medal, coming fourth in the 400 metres, she decided to cheer him up by entering the 800. Brightwell later won a silver medal in the 400 metres relay. Britain's fourth gold came in the 20 kilometres walk where Ken Matthews was the favourite to win gold which he duly did in a new Olympic record time. Despite his long record of achievement in his sport Ken Matthews was the only one of the four gold medallists who was not recognized in the 1965 New Year Honours list, the others all receiving an MBE. This injustice, which does not appear to have worried Matthews in the least, was finally rectified in 1978.

Two of the most remarkable competitors were to be found in the US team. Joe Frazier was the second-string fighter in the American team for the heavyweight division but won the gold medal despite fighting with a broken thumb in the semi-final and final. He later won the world heavyweight professional championship, fighting some memorable bouts against Muhammad Ali. The greatest surprise came in the 10,000 metres event where the first ever American victory at that distance was achieved by the unknown American Billy Mills who, despite his name, was a Sioux Indian.

At Tokyo 93 nations were represented by 4,451 male and 682 female competitors.

# Mexico City 1968
*Altitude and Black Power*

A t the Summer Olympics (the only ones held to date in Latin America, Rio de Janeiro will be following in 2016), East and West Germany competed as separate teams for the first time but before the Games even began an attempt by Mexican students to protest against their authoritarian government in front of the world's media covering the games ended in disaster. A demonstration by students in a district of Mexico City ten days before the games began was harshly suppressed and 200 demonstrators were shot, many of them killed. However, the main feature of the Mexico Games concerned the fact that they took place more than 7,000 feet above sea level where the thin atmosphere presented severe problems for competitors in endurance events, like the great Australian runner Ron Clarke who, having set 17 world records, was expected to win the 5,000 and 10,000 metres races. Clarke collapsed and nearly died from altitude sickness in the latter race, probably suffering damage to his heart which caused long-term health problems. He later enjoyed a successful career in Australian politics. The endurance events were dominated by African runners from high-altitude countries, gaining medals in all events from 800 metres to the Marathon. However, in 'explosive' events like sprints and jumping, records tumbled. Bob Beamon of the USA broke the long jump record set by Jesse Owens by such a long distance, more than half a metre, that he jumped past the measuring apparatus at the pit and an additional steel measure had to be

*Fosbury Flop*

found. His jump remained a world record until 1991. Mexico also saw the first appearance, in the high jump, of the 'Fosbury Flop' which involved executing the jump head first with the athlete's back arched above the bar. The architect of the new technique, Dick Fosbury of the USA, duly broke the high jump record. A somewhat similar technique had, of course, been ruled illegal when used by Babe Didrikson at Los Angeles in 1932.

---

### THE MAN IN BLACK
*The Winter Olympics of 1968 took place in Grenoble, France and soon became a source of controversy since the Olympic authorities forbade the competitors to use equipment displaying the names of commercial organizations. The skiers protested*

*since they were dependent upon
'sponsors' to supply them with
equipment. The authorities backed
down, thereby opening a crack in
the door of amateurism through
which many would later pass. The
French skier Jean-Claude Killy won
three gold medals but only after a
controversy involving the Austrian
competitor Karl Schranz who
claimed that during the slalom race
a mysterious 'man in black' crossed
his path. Schranz was allowed a
re-run and posted the fastest time but
was subsequently disqualified when
television footage showed that he had
missed a gate on his first run.*

In the final of the 100 metres all
the runners, for the first time, were
black athletes. Tommie Smith and
John Carlos of the USA won the
gold and bronze medals respectively
and then caused a sensation by their
behaviour on the rostrum during
the medal presentation ceremony.
This was the era of the American
Civil Rights movement when black
Americans were asserting their rights
to vote, to attend schools with white
classmates and to sit where they
wished on public transport. Earlier
in 1968 Martin Luther King had
been gunned down after leading a
Civil Rights demonstration and the
campaign was finely balanced. As the
American anthem was played and
the Stars and Stripes were raised to
celebrate the triumph of the two
black athletes, instead of placing
their hands on their hearts as was
the custom, Smith raised his black-
gloved right hand, and Carlos his
black-gloved left hand, in a clenched
fist 'black power' salute to remind the
watching audience of their second-
class status in their own country.
The two men were suspended from
the games and expelled from the
Olympic Village, but they had made
their point and the discriminatory
rules and practices from which they
(and Jesse Owens before them)
had suffered were removed under
President Richard Nixon over the
next four years.

At Mexico City, for the first
time more than a hundred nations
were represented. 112 nations were
represented by 4,724 and 774 female
competitors.

# Munich 1972
## *An Olympic Tragedy*

The 1972 Winter Olympics were held at Sapporo, Japan, the first Winter Games held in Asia. Controversy again struck when the Austrian skier Karl Schranz (whose behaviour during the 1968 Olympics has been noted above) was banned by Avery Brundage, President of the IOC, having received $50,000 in sponsorship from equipment suppliers. In response the Canadians refused to enter an ice hockey team because of the blatant professionalism of competitors from the Soviet bloc to which Brundage turned a blind eye. The Munich Summer Olympics, which started so promisingly, are remembered for the most tragic event ever to hit the games: the so-called 'Munich Massacre'. The German authorities, anxious to expunge the memory of the 1936 Nazi-dominated Berlin Games, adopted the slogan 'the Happy Games' and produced the first Olympic mascot in the form of a dachshund called 'Waldi'. And the opening ceremony on 26th August, watched for the first time by a TV

audience exceeding one billion, set the games off to a good start with the Olympic Oath taken for the first time by a young woman, Heidi Schuller. However, on 5 September eight Palestinian guerrillas from the 'Black September' group broke into the Israeli quarters and took as hostages 11 athletes, officials and coaches, two of the Israelis being shot dead as they resisted. The group was then transferred to Munich airport to board a plane for an unspecified Arab country but a botched rescue attempt led to the deaths of all the hostages and all but three of the guerrillas, who were later released from captivity by the West German authorities in exchange for a Lufthansa jet which had been hijacked. Two of the three guerrillas were later hunted down and killed by the Israeli secret service Mossad. High levels of security were

*Munich 1972*

*Mark Spitz*

henceforth a feature of all Olympic Games. The third guerrilla remains at large, no doubt on Mossad's hit list and beset by feelings of anxiety.

The undoubted star of the Munich Olympics was the American swimmer Mark Spitz who had been swimming for 75 minutes a day since he was eight years old. Having promised to win six golds at Mexico City he disappointed himself and others with only two but finally showed what he could do by winning seven golds at Munich, giving a total of nine. Only the American swimmer Michael Phelps has won more, with a haul of 14 at Athens and Beijing. After the Munich massacre Spitz, who was of Jewish descent, was thought to be a prime target and security around him was stepped up before he returned to the USA. However, more public attention was centred on the Soviet

gymnastic team and in particular on Olga Korbut. Five feet high, a little over six stone in weight and 17 years old she won three gold medals and one silver. Her performance on the floor exercise won the hearts of spectators who booed for five minutes when she was awarded a mark of only 9.8 on the vault. She was the first person ever to execute a backward somersault on the beam. She retired from gymnastics and became a popular singer in a group in her native Belarus before emigrating to the USA where she now lives. The great Finnish distance runner Lasse Viren followed Zatopek and Kuts in winning both the 5,000 and 10,000 metres events, as he was to do again in Montreal four years later.

## GOLDEN GIRLS, AND BOYS
*The Soviet gymnast Larisa Latynina holds the record for the greatest number of medals won. Between 1956 and 1964 she won 18 medals of which nine were gold. Nikolay Andrianov, also a Soviet gymnast, took 15 medals between 1972 and 1980 of which seven were gold but*

*the swimmer Michael Phelps of the USA is the most successful winner of gold medals with 14 in 2004 and 2008, plus two bronze. Remarkably the record for athletic titles is still held by Raymond Ewry of the USA who, between 1900 and 1908, took first place on ten occasions in the standing high jump, the standing long jump, the long jump and the triple jump, the first two events no longer featuring in competition.*

---

Britain's star for the games was 33-year-old Mary Peters. Born in Merseyside and brought up in Belfast, she described herself in unflattering terms: 'Mary Rand is Queen of the naturals; I'm Queen of the triers.' She won the women's pentathlon by a narrow margin from the German favourite but not everyone was pleased. This was at the height of the sectarian troubles in Northern Ireland and her life was threatened if she returned to Belfast. Her father had emigrated to Australia many years before but, to her delight and surprise, returned to greet her after the medal presentation ceremony. She became Dame Mary Peters in the New Year's

Honours List for 2000.

There were disputes elsewhere. An American swimmer called Rick De Mont, having won the 400 metres freestyle, was disqualified for taking a drug to combat his asthma which would almost certainly have been allowed if he had made known his intentions beforehand. There was more controversy in the 400 metres track event where another 'black power' protest by the black American athletes who had won the gold and silver medals led to their being banned. The Americans were therefore unable to field a 4 x 400 metres relay team. One of the loudest cheers of the games occurred when a German spectator, who had joined the Marathon shortly before the runners entered the Olympic stadium, was mistaken by the predominantly German crowd for the winner. Frank Shorter of the USA who won the Marathon was no doubt surprised to find someone ahead of him at this late stage but was reassured to hear an American TV commentator call out 'It's a fraud, Frank.'

## THE HEAD WAITER

More embarrassment but less offence was caused by the USA's Dave Wottle. He habitually wore a golf cap during races and waited until the last moment before bursting into the lead over the final stretch. These characteristics earned him the name 'The Head Waiter'. Having won the 800 metres gold Wottle forgot to remove his trademark cap during the medal ceremony as the 'Star-Spangled Banner' was played and the Stars and Stripes climbed the flagpole. He promptly apologized to everyone, beginning with his colonel!

## OLDEST, TALLEST AND BIGGEST

*In the equestrian team's dressage event Britain's Lorna Johnstone became the oldest ever competitor for Great Britain, reaching the last 12 at the age of 70 years and 5 days. At seven feet four inches, Tommy Burleson of the USA became the tallest medallist with a silver in, as one would expect, basketball.*

An American, Chris Taylor, became the heaviest medal winner when he gained a silver medal in Munich at wrestling, weighing in at over 28 stone.

At Munich 121 nations were represented by 6,062 male and 1,059 female competitors.

## LORD KILLANIN, IOC PRESIDENT 1972–80

*Michael Morris, Baron Killanin, (1914–99) was born in London of Irish descent and educated at Eton and Cambridge where he became president of the celebrated Footlights dramatic society. He later became a journalist and was elected President of the Olympic Council of Ireland in 1950. His choice as sixth President of the IOC appears to have owed much to the fact that he had not offended anyone, as other candidates had, and was regarded as innocuous. Brundage, his predecessor, was credited with the comment, 'We need a leader and Michael isn't one.' His presidency was marked by the financial problems of the Montreal Games and the boycotts of the Moscow Olympics.*

# THE ERA OF BOYCOTTS

## Montreal 1976
*Boycotts and near bankruptcy*

The Montreal Games of 1976 achieved a number of unwanted distinctions. They were the first Olympics which were boycotted on a large scale over the issue of apartheid. Led by Tanzania, 31 nations boycotted the games, mostly African states who were protesting at the participation of New Zealand whose rugby team had recently played against South Africa. One of the principal losers from the boycott was Tanzania's own Filbert Bayi who had recently lost his 1500 metres and mile world records to New Zealand's John Walker and now lost the best opportunity he would ever have to win them back. Walker duly won the gold medal in the 1500 metres. Taiwan withdrew because, to pacify the Chinese who were now full members of the United Nations Security Council, the Taiwanese were not allowed to fly their flag or play their anthem. Nine days before the scheduled date for the opening ceremony this refusal looked as if it might lead to the cancellation of the Games altogether but a compromise was stitched together over protests from Taiwan. The loss of athletes and visitors that the boycotts caused compounded the financial problems of the Montreal authorities. An initial budget for the games of $310 million climbed relentlessly to more than $1,400 million as construction workers, sensing the strength of their bargaining position as deadlines approached, mounted a series of strikes for better pay. Further financial problems arose from the need for better security arrangements following the massacre of Israeli athletes at Munich. The combination of mounting costs and falling visitor

*Montreal's very expensive stadium*

numbers came close to bankrupting this prosperous Canadian city whose citizens finally paid off the debt through their rates and local taxes in December 2006, 30 years after the conclusion of the games. Future Olympics outside the Communist bloc, starting with the Los Angeles Games of 1984, would be funded not only by long-suffering taxpayers but also by heavy infusions of commercial sponsorship which became available as worldwide television coverage of the events expanded rapidly after 1976.

## INNSBRUCK AGAIN, BUT STILL NO CANADIANS

*Innsbruck in Austria hosted the 1976 Winter Olympics for the second time, having done so for the games of 1964. Denver was originally chosen as the host city but withdrew when its electors baulked at the cost, the only city in history to have turned down the chance to host the Olympic Games. How the citizens of Montreal must have wished they had been so wise! The Innsbruck Games of 1976 were noted for the fact that Britain won a rare Winter gold through the skater Robin Curry and Canada once again refused to send an ice hockey team in protest against the sham amateur status of Soviet bloc teams.*

Nor was there any comfort in the performance of the Canadian team. For the only time in Olympic history the host nation failed to win a single gold medal while the best that Great Britain could do in athletics was a bronze medal, won by Brendan Foster in the 10,000 metres final, though in the heats he had the satisfaction of setting a new world record which stood until 1984. In 1981 he founded the Great North Run on his native Tyneside which regularly attracts 50,000 runners a year, exceeding the numbers participating in the London Marathon. Although the Canadians enjoyed no financial or athletic success they were able to celebrate a romantic success following the opening ceremony. The Olympic flame was lit by two young Canadians: Sandra Henderson of British stock and Stephane Prefontaine who was French Canadian, this gesture symbolizing the unity of the two communities, a unity which had not always been evident. The two young people later married. The Romanian gymnast Nadia Comaneci won three gold medals at Montreal and became noted for the fact that it was very difficult to make her smile (in contrast to Olga Korbut who smiled all the time at Munich). But then, living in Ceaucescu's Romania she had even less than Olga Korbut to smile about. She won two further golds at Moscow, defected to the USA shortly before the fall of the Ceaucescu regime and still lives there. She was the first gymnast to gain a perfect score of 10, a score with which the Olympic scoreboard was unable to cope.

## PRESSING THE WRONG BUTTON
*Boris Onishchenko, representing the Soviet Union in the Modern Pentathlon, was found to have used, in the fencing section of the event, an épée which had a button on the pommel which, when pressed, would record a hit on his opponent whether or not he had made contact. He was disqualified, together with the entire Soviet pentathlon team.*

Lasse Viren repeated his victories in the 5,000 and 10,000 metres, the latter to Brendan Foster's cost, though on this occasion his victory was slightly marred by the question of 'blood doping', a process by which a quantity of blood is removed from an athlete, treated in such a way as to enhance the levels of red blood cells which carry oxygen, and then transfused back into the athlete before competition. It was suggested that Viren had adopted this practice but it was a very difficult process to detect at the time and by no means clear that it was illegal – it was, after all, the athlete's own blood. Since the 1980s the hormone erythropoietin has been injected into athletes' bloodstreams to improve oxygen levels. This is definitely illegal and means have been found to detect it, some athletes being banned as a result.

## THE SOVIET FEMALE GIANT
*In 1976 the Soviet team won the first ever female Olympic basketball competition, beating the favourites the USA by an embarrassing 112-77 points in the semi-final. They were*

*helped by the presence of Juliana Semenova who, at seven feet two inches, was the tallest woman ever to take part in the competition.*
*At Montreal 92 nations were represented by 4,785 male and 1,258 female competitors.*

## Moscow 1980
*More boycotts*

By the time that Moscow hosted the Olympics in 1980 the Games had become firmly established as a weapon in the Cold War. In 1979 the Soviet Union, under the increasingly senile rule of Leonid Brezhnev, was tricked into invading Afghanistan by some clever American propaganda suggesting that the regime, sympathetic to Moscow, was being undermined. The Soviets had fallen into a trap which not only consumed much blood and treasure which its ailing economy could ill afford but also provided the USA with a wonderful propaganda weapon. In a show of wonderfully righteous indignation the USA demanded a boycott of the forthcoming Moscow

Olympics which was observed by over 40 states including Germany, Japan and of course the USA itself, all of them important Olympic nations. At this time there was a good deal of agitation in Poland, an increasingly reluctant member of the Soviet bloc, leading eventually to the growth of the 'Solidarity' trade union led by Lech Walesa. The winner of the gold medal in the pole vault was the Polish athlete Wladyslaw Kozakiewicz who seized the opportunity to defy the Russian crowd who were already disappointed at his defeat of their own champion. He gave them the 'Bras d'Honneur' which involves bending one arm into an L shape while gripping the inside of the bent arm with the other hand. It is insulting and could be described as meaning 'up yours'. It had the intended effect of insulting and enraging the crowd as well as annoying the IOC but he was allowed to keep his gold medal.

Great Britain did not boycott the games despite the urgings of the pro-American Prime Minister Margaret Thatcher, a decision which ensured the participation of two of Britain's greatest ever athletes, Steve Ovett and Sebastian Coe. In Olympic events, some of which were undoubtedly devalued by the absence of the USA, Britain won gold medals for the 100 metres (Allan Wells); the 800 metres (Steve Ovett); the 1500 metres (Sebastian Coe); the decathlon (Daley Thompson); and the 100 metres breaststroke (Duncan Goodhew). Allan Wells' sprint gold was the first won by a Briton since Harold Abrahams at Paris in 1924 and Daley Thompson was the first

*Steve Ovett*

*Daley Thompson*

British winner of the decathlon, a triumph he was to repeat in Los Angeles four years later. Since Coe and Ovett were the two outstanding middle distance runners of their generation, setting 14 world records between them, there is little reason to believe that participation by the boycotting nations would have made any difference to the events in which they competed. But all did not go according to plan. Coe was expected to beat Ovett in the 800 metres, his best distance, but had to settle for the silver medal behind his great rival. The distress on Coe's face as he received 'only' the silver medal on the podium will not be forgotten by those who witnessed it. But he gained his revenge in the 1500 metres event, winning comfortably while Ovett settled for the bronze.

## SMALL BUT TOUGH
*The North Korean gymnast Choe Myong-Lui was the smallest ever Olympic competitor at Moscow, measuring four feet five inches and weighing 55 pounds (less than four stone). In comparison Lu Li of China was a giant, measuring half an inch taller and 79 pounds, a whole five stone and nine pounds. But then she did win gold on the asymmetrical bars at Barcelona in 1992.*

## LAKE PLACID AGAIN
As in 1932, Lake Placid, New York State, was the setting for the Winter Olympics and on this occasion no risks were taken with the climate, artificial snow being provided in case of unsuitable weather. Despite the forthcoming boycott of the Moscow Games, already called for by President Carter, the Soviet Union and its allies took part as did the People's Republic of China (i.e. Communist China) for the first time. They won no medals but they had come to stay and participated in future Olympics. Robin Cousins followed Robin Curry four years earlier in winning another gold medal for Great Britain, in figure skating. Controversy surrounded the plan to convert the Olympic accommodation into a prison, especially when the Prisons Construction Service won a court judgment to allow it to use the Olympic symbol on a poster! At Moscow 80 nations were represented by 4,149 male and 1,134 female competitors.

# Juan Antonio Samaranch, IOC President, 1980–2001

*The Order of the Golden Fleece: 'beyond the dreams of avarice'*

In 1980, following the controversial and much-boycotted Moscow Olympics, the Spanish grandee Juan Antonio Samaranch (1920–2010) first Marquis of Samaranch, was elected 7th IOC President. His presidency was as active and controversial as that of his predecessor, Lord Killanin, had been passive and innocuous. His tenure of 21 years was second only to that of Pierre de Coubertin and the IOC had to amend its rules to make it possible. He inherited an organization that was very short of money and dogged by controversies over boycotts, professionalism and the growing problems of drugs. When he left office in 2001 he left the Olympic Games as one of the most coveted trophies any city could win and rich beyond the dreams of avarice.

His background was not without controversy. Born into a wealthy Catalan family in Barcelona he was conscripted into the Republican forces during the Spanish civil war but, lacking sympathy for the Republican cause, he fled to France and returned to Spain after Franco's victory, joining the 'Falange' and being appointed by the Spanish dictator to a government post in charge of sport. By the time that Franco died Samaranch had led Spanish teams to the Olympics several times and was vice-president of the IOC and one of Spain's better-known personalities on the international stage. The new democratic government of Spain sent him into a comfortable exile as the nation's first ambassador to Moscow (1977–80) where his diplomatic skills and personal charm enabled him to convert his former Communist friends into allies who helped him to become IOC President. The boycotts by the Soviet bloc of the Los Angeles Games were a setback but the disappointment was more than offset by the realization that sponsorship and the sale of television rights, as exemplified at Los Angeles, could make the Olympics a very attractive and profitable proposition. It was during his period of office that the bidding process for the Olympics became fiercely competitive and it is no coincidence that the first serious bribery scandal arose during this time, over the Salt Lake City Winter Olympics, though Samaranch himself was not directly involved.

## TV RULES

*The importance of TV revenue to the Olympics may be seen from the following table which sets out the revenue from broadcast rights in millions of US $:*

|  | Summer Games | Winter Games |
|---|---|---|
| *Moscow / Lake Placid 1980* | 101 | 21 |
| *Los Angeles / Sarajevo 1984* | 287 | 103 |
| *Seoul / Calgary 1988* | 403 | 325 |
| *Barcelona / Albertville 1992* | 636 | 292 |
| *Atlanta 1996 / Lillehammer 1994* | 935 | 353 |
| *Sydney 2000 / Nagano 1998* | 1,332 | 513 |
| *Athens 2004 / Salt Lake City 2002* | 1,498 | 738 |
| *Beijing 2008 / Turin 2006* | 1,715 | 832 |
| *London 2012 / Vancouver 2010 (est.)* | 3,000 | 900 |

*In addition, the Olympics sponsorship programme raises about $1 billion for the Games.*

In 2001 Samaranch, bedecked with honours from many nations ranging from Georgia's Order of the Golden Fleece to Ukraine's Order of Prince Yaroslav the Wise (Third Class), retired from the presidency at the age of 81. He had had to cope with boycotts, drugs and bribery allegations but left the Olympics the Greatest (and possibly the wealthiest) Show on Earth, its only serious challenger being the World Cup for football whose own governing body, FIFA, remains beset with its own problems of corruption.

# Los Angeles 1984
*Television to the rescue*

Los Angeles gained the 1984 Olympics by default. After the financial disasters that beset Montreal, cities were circumspect about bidding for the games and the only other city which expressed interest, Tehran, withdrew following the revolution which overthrew the Iranian Shah and plunged the nation into turmoil. Los Angeles was fortified by the knowledge that much of the infrastructure of the 1932 Olympics remained in place and could be refurbished at modest cost. A new swimming pool and cycling velodrome were paid for by corporate sponsors. The organizers were further emboldened by the confidence that

*Los Angeles stadium 1984*

they would earn much from the sale of television rights which drew in the then colossal sum of $287 million, though this would be dwarfed by future games. Amateurism at the Olympics was drawing its last breath and in 1986 the requirement that participants be amateurs was removed from the Olympic Charter. Politics still cast its shadow. Moscow was still smarting from the American boycott of its games over the Afghan conflict which was still going on and on 8 May, 1984, less than three months before the games were due to begin and on the day the Olympic flame reached the USA, the Soviet Union and 14 other Eastern bloc countries announced that they would boycott them (but excluding Romania who, to most people's surprise, came second in the medals table after the USA). Iran and Libya boycotted the games for different reasons. The torch relay passed through 33 states, covered over 9,000 miles and used 3,616 runners, one of them the noted athlete O.J. Simpson who was soon to become known for less happy reasons and another being Bill Thorpe, grandson of Jim 'the greatest athlete in the world' Thorpe of the Stockholm Games who had died in 1953, having been pardoned for his 'professionalism' in 1982. At the opening ceremony the torch was borne by Gina Hemphill, the granddaughter of Jesse Owens, who had died in 1980.

## SARAJEVO

*The Yugoslav city of Sarajevo in Bosnia was the scene of the Winter Olympics. This quiet, peaceful little community was chiefly remembered as the scene of the assassination of Archduke Franz Ferdinand of Austria which prompted the outbreak of World War I but in the 1990s it became a scene of tragedy as Serbian forces laid siege to it, wrecking the city and killing many inhabitants. The Sarajevo Winter Olympics were notable in Great Britain for the gold medal in ice skating won by Jayne Torvill and Christopher Dean to the tune of Ravel's 'Bolero'.*

There were some notable achievements by competitors who would achieve lasting fame. Carl Lewis made his Olympic debut,

matching the four golds won by Jesse Owns in the 100 and 200 metres, the long jump and the 4 × 100 metres relay. Carlos Lopes of Portugal won his country's first ever gold medal in the Marathon and in so doing set a record of 2 hours, 9 minutes 21 seconds that would stand for 24 years and interrupted the long reign in the event of African runners from high altitudes. Britain won five gold medals, including the first of five in successive Olympics for the rower Steve Redgrave, a record unmatched for an endurance event. Sebastian Coe again won the 1500 metres and gained another silver in the 800 metres, and Daley Thompson again took the decathlon, setting a new world record. China won its first ever gold medal, thus announcing its arrival on the world stage on which it would become a dominant influence over the next 25 years. One of the great surprises was the popularity of football, a game widely played by amateurs in the USA but scarcely known as a professional game. Stadiums were packed for most of the matches in the 100,000-seater Pasadena Rose Bowl, France beating

Brazil 2-0 in the final. This interest led to the USA staging the 1994 World Cup. There were some strange results, notably in the swimming pool where two finals were staged for the 4 × 400 metres freestyle relay: one for those who had qualified for the final and another, the 'B' final, to console those who had been eliminated in earlier rounds. The 'B' final was won in a faster time than that achieved by the gold medal winners and set a new Olympic record. The greatest controversy occurred in the final of the women's 3000 metres when Zola Budd, a South African representing Great Britain and running barefoot as she always did, was leading the race. The American favourite Mary Decker collided with Zola, tripped and fell, ending her part in the race. Zola faded to the sound of booing from the crowd, finishing seventh though she was later adjudged to be innocent of any offence. A more sinister note was struck when 12 competitors were disqualified for doping offences – a sign of things to come.

## DRUGS

*Drugs have been a feature of the Olympics at least since 1968 when the first competitor was disqualified though there were suspicions since the late 1950s that some athletes, especially women from the Eastern bloc, were unnaturally muscular. At Munich in 1972 seven athletes were disqualified; in 1976 at Montreal 11; in Moscow 1980, none; Los Angeles 1984, 12; Seoul 1988, 11; Barcelona 1992, five; Atlanta 1996, two; Sydney 2000, ten; Athens 2004, 14 plus nine who failed tests before competition began and never got as far as the start line.*

*At Los Angeles 140 nations were represented by 5,233 male and 1,575 female competitors.*

# THE PROFESSIONALS ARRIVE AND TV TAKES HOLD

## Seoul, 1988
*Troublesome neighbours*

*TV Screen*

In 1988 South Korea was still technically at war with its northern neighbour (as it still is) and the Communist North boycotted the games as did its hardline allies Albania and Cuba, though of the three only Cuba had any pretensions to sporting achievement. These were the last Olympics at which the two athletic superpowers the Soviet Union and East Germany competed, since by the time the Barcelona Olympics opened, the Berlin Wall had been gleefully pulled down by Berliners from both sides, Germany was reunited and the Soviet Union and its empire had vanished, unmourned, into history. The end of mass boycotts connected with the Cold War and the matter of apartheid in South Africa meant that, despite the tense relationship between the two Koreas and the security fears this engendered, a record 159 nations attended and, as at Los Angeles, the sale of TV rights (for $403 million) was critical to the success of the Games and to some extent dictated the scheduling of popular events. Since the amendment of the Olympic Charter in 1986 professional athletes were now accepted without demur so there was no further need for pretences about athletics scholarships or military sinecures. The Koreans, noting that the original Olympic banner was by now rather tattered, presented the IOC with a new one made from Korean silk. The torch was carried into the Olympic stadium by the Korean Kitei Son who had won the Marathon at Berlin in 1936 having been compelled, against his will, to compete for Japan which at the time was occupying his country.

## CALGARY

*The Winter Olympics were held in Calgary, Canada and are chiefly remembered for the exploits of Britain's Michael 'Eddie the Eagle' Edwards who, with minimal support and rather poor equipment, managed to break the British record with a ski jump of 71 metres while coming last, some 20 metres behind the rest of the field. Long after the medal winners are forgotten he is still remembered with affection and some admiration as one who struggled against adversity, without success as normally measured. The Jamaican bobsleigh team also deserve to be remembered. They crashed at their first attempt at a run, allegedly never having raced on snow before!*

The star of the Seoul Games was the American athlete Florence Griffith-Joyner, known as 'Flo-Jo'. Noted for her colourful celebrity and dress sense and her even more colourful fingernails, she was a personality as well as an athlete when she arrived in Seoul where she won gold in the 100 and 200 metres (setting records in both) and 4 × 100 metres relay; and silver in the 4 × 400 metres relay. She retired after Seoul amidst rumours that her performances were drug-assisted though she never failed a test. She died in her sleep in 1998 at the age of only 38 of an epileptic seizure and the post-mortem found that she had been suffering from a brain abnormality. Tennis returned to the Olympics after an interval of 64 years, enabling Germany's Steffi Graf to add an Olympic gold medal to her tally of Grand Slams (including Wimbledon that year) and replace the great Helen Wills Moody who had been reigning champion since Paris, 1924. Nevertheless there were many who doubted the value of taking into the Olympic Games sports like tennis and football which already had their own well-established and more significant competitions. The Seoul Games had one hero and one particularly conspicuous villain. The hero was Canadian Lawrence Lemieux who was heading for a silver medal in sailing when he abandoned the race to rescue an injured competitor who was in danger. Lemieux finished in 21st place and was given the Pierre de Coubertin Medal in recognition of his sacrifice and his courage.

## THE PIERRE DE COUBERTIN MEDAL

*This award has only been made 11 times and recognizes sportsmanship rather than victories. Recipients include Luz Long (posthumously) who advised Jesse Owens to adjust his run-up in the long jump at the Berlin Olympics of 1936, advice which cost him the gold medal; and Vanderlei de Lima of Brazil who was leading the Marathon in Athens in 2004 when he was obstructed by a spectator, eventually winning the bronze. A Brazilian beach volleyball player who had won a gold medal offered his medal to de Lima but de Lima handed it back, explaining that his medal, though made of bronze, was gold to him.*

The conspicuous villain was another Canadian, the sprinter Ben Johnson who, having won the 100 metres in a world record time, was disqualified for taking performance-enhancing drugs, the first really high-profile disqualification in Olympic history. Nine other competitors were disqualified for the same reason, mostly in weightlifting, but they are scarcely remembered. Further controversy occurred in the boxing ring where Park Si-Hun of the host nation South Korea was awarded the gold medal in the light-middleweight division despite his American opponent Roy Jones landing 86 blows to Park's 32. The three judges who voted against Jones were later suspended and according to some accounts Park apologized to Jones. In East Germany's final appearance as a separate nation its athlete Christa Luding-Rothenburge became the only athlete ever to win medals at Winter and Summer Olympics in the same year, winning a gold for speed skating in Calgary and then a silver for cycling at Seoul.

## CAN'T GET ENOUGH OF IT

*At Seoul Kerstin Palm, a Swedish fencer, became the first woman to take part in seven Olympics, her best result coming in 1968 when she finished fifth. Since then four women have matched her achievement, as have six men. Multiple Olympians are most common in shooting, sailing, fencing and equestrianism. Austrian sailor Hubert Raudaschl (two silver medals) and Canadian equestrian Ian Millar (one silver medal) have both recorded nine Olympic appearances and Millar would have recorded ten but for the Canadian boycott of Moscow. But he's still in the saddle, so watch this space! No-one, however, can equal Steve Redgrave's five golds in successive Olympic endurance events.*

*At Seoul 159 nations were represented by 6,259 male and 2,214 female competitors.*

# Paralympics take flight
*'An integrated whole'*

A t Seoul, for the first time, the word 'Paralympic' was applied to the Games for disabled athletes and, again for the first time, these Games immediately followed the Summer Olympics. They are not, however,

the only events associated with the Olympic Games which have involved people with disabilities. In 1924 Paris, host to the 'Chariots of Fire' Olympics, staged the 'Deaflympics' for those with hearing deficiencies. This spanned 16 individual sports including athletics, badminton and cycling together with four team sports – basketball, football, volleyball and beach volleyball. These were held every four years, albeit separately from the Summer Olympics, and have since been subsumed in the Paralympic movement. In 2001 the IOC and the International Paralympic Committee (IPC) agreed that thenceforth cities chosen for the Games would stage both the Olympics and Paralympics. The philosophy was expressed by Sebastian Coe speaking of the 2012 London Olympics: 'We want to change public attitudes towards disability, celebrate the excellence of Paralympic sport and enshrine from the very outset that the two Games are an integrated whole.' No individual better symbolizes this aim than the swimmer Eleanor ('Ellie') Simmonds who won two gold medals at the Beijing Olympics followed by the BBC Young Sports Personality of the Year award and, in 2009 aged 14, became the youngest person ever to receive an MBE from the Queen in the New Year's Honours list.

The Paralympians have developed six categories within which competitions are held. These are amputees; cerebral palsy; intellectual disabilities; wheelchair users; visually impaired; and an 'other' category which includes dwarfism, multiple sclerosis and congenital deformities. Oscar 'the Blade Runner' Pistorius, the South African runner who had both his legs amputated below the knee, runs with two carbon-fibre blades and won gold in the 100, 200 and 400 metres races in the Beijing Paralympics. He applied to compete in the regular Summer Games at Beijing. A good deal of controversy surrounds the question of whether his carbon-fibre blades give him an advantage over other athletes and after some hesitation and several scientific tests he was told he could compete if he reached the Olympic qualifying time which he narrowly failed to do. He may yet qualify for London 2012. Further controversy on matters such as the technology of

disability advances may confidently be anticipated. The Olympic and Paralympic competitions are not mutually exclusive. Sighted guides for blind athletes are considered to be part of the team and can qualify for medals. Neroli Fairhall, a wheelchair-bound archer from New Zealand, won gold at the 1980 Olympics and went on to become the first Paralympian to compete in the Summer Olympics at Los Angeles, though she did not gain a medal. Television coverage of the Paralympics advanced slowly, beginning with some tapes at Montreal in 1976. Live coverage began at Barcelona in 1992 and gathered pace at Sydney where the Paralympics reached a global audience of 300 million. There have been a number of cases of cheating. In 2000 it was discovered that several members of the Spanish gold-medal winning team in the basketball competition for the intellectually disabled did not qualify as such and in 2008 at Beijing three weightlifters and a basketball player were excluded after tests for banned substances. It could be argued that this is evidence that the

Paralympics have really arrived on the sporting scene! The most successful Paralympian is the blind swimmer Trischa Zorn of the USA who has won 55 medals of which 41 are gold. She would almost certainly have competed in the Summer Olympics at Moscow with the full US team but for the boycott.

archer, Antonio Rebollo, fired a blazing arrow into the torch, setting it ablaze and marking the beginning of the games. Linford Christie became the third Briton to win the 100 metres, following Harold Abrahams and Alan Wells at the ripe old age, for a sprinter, of 32 while Sally Gunnell won the women's 400 metre hurdles..

## Barcelona 1992
*Triumph for the 'Unified Team' (?)*

The collapse of the Soviet Union (and later of Yugoslavia) led to a gradual increase in the number of independent nations competing in the Olympics from 1992 onwards. A 'Unified Team' representing the 'Confederation of Independent States' entered with athletes from Russia, Belarus, Ukraine, Kazakhstan and Uzbekistan, though these last four would soon join the Baltic states of Estonia, Latvia and Lithuania in entering separate teams. Much was made of the fact that one of the early chariot races in the Ancient Games was won by Lucius Minicius, a native of Barcelona, and a spectacular effect was achieved when a Paralympic

*Sally Gunnell*

ALBERTVILLE, 1992
*In 1992 Albertville, in France, became the smallest place ever to host the Winter Olympic Games and also the last to stage them in the same year as the Summer Olympics. Thereafter the Winter Games were 'intercalated', being held in the even year before the Summer Olympics. Annelise Coberger, a New Zealand skier, won the southern hemisphere's*

*first Winter Olympic medal in the slalom. The national medal count was headed by Germany with ten golds followed by Norway who, with nine golds, demonstrated what you can achieve with a cold climate and a lot of snow even if your population is small in number.*

## MEDAL TABLES

*In 1992 at Barcelona the 'Unified Team' topped the medals on the only occasion that it entered. The USA has topped the Olympic medals tables on more occasions (15) than all other nations taken together, beginning in 1896. They are followed by the Soviet Union and its successor the Confederation of Independent States (seven, falling between 1956 and 1992); with one each for France (1900), Britain (1908), Germany (1936), and China (2008).*

*At Barcelona 169 nations were represented by 6,656 male and 2,712 female competitors.*

# Atlanta 1996
## *The Coca-Cola Games*

Atlanta won the right to host the 1996 games despite a strong challenge from Athens which believed that, as the original home of the Olympics, Greece should host the games on the hundredth anniversary of the first Modern Olympics. Athens actually won more votes than Atlanta in the first ballot but as other contenders were eliminated (including Toronto, Melbourne and Manchester) Atlanta emerged as the winner. The Atlanta Games represented a further move towards commercial sponsorship which was perhaps inevitable in the city which is the home of Coca-Cola who, for a handsome fee, secured the exclusive right to provide its drinks at Olympic venues. A series of disputes arose between the IOC and the city authorities over the sale of advertising and of licences for street vendors to sell products which were not official sponsors and the opening ceremony, featuring 500 attractive cheerleaders, was criticized as garish – though it was also fun. Television rights were sold for a new record sum, $935 million. An early proposal to construct a swimming pool in the shape of a hamburger was swiftly dismissed (the line had to be drawn somewhere!) but the official view of the IOC was perhaps best summed up by its President, Juan Antonio Samaranch, who, at the closing ceremony, restricted himself to saying that the Games had been 'most exceptional' rather than his previous practice of calling them 'the best ever', a practice he resumed four years later at Sydney. On the other hand Atlanta could console itself with the fact that it made a profit of $10 million from the games. Speculation over who would light the Olympic flame was ended with the appearance of Muhammad Ali, the most famous sportsman in the world, who performed the ceremony despite suffering from the effects of Parkinson's Disease. Security was tight but not tight enough to prevent a bomb exploding in a city park, killing two and injuring over a hundred. In 2003 Eric Rudolph was arrested and confessed to the crime following a long period on the FBI's 'Most Wanted' list despite his family's belief

*Muhammad Ali*

that he was innocent, a conviction demonstrated by his brother who videoed himself cutting off his own hand in order, in his own words, to 'send a message to the FBI and the media'. Rudolph also confessed to other similar crimes which were motivated by homophobia and opposition to abortion.

## A MINUTE FOR SARAJEVO

*The Winter Olympics were held at Lillehammer, Norway in 1994, two years earlier than the Summer Games. From this time on the Winter Games would always be 'intercalated' in this way. At the opening ceremony a minute's silence was observed for former hosts, the city of Sarajevo, under siege from Serb forces. The Lillehammer Games became known for the attempt by the US skater Tonya Harding to gain an advantage over her figure-skating compatriot Nancy Kerrigan by conniving at an attack on Nancy which left her bruised but still able to compete. Nancy won the silver medal while Tonya Harding won opprobrium.*

---

The most moving story to emerge from Atlanta was that of Josiah Thugwane who represented his native South Africa at the second Olympics after the nation's return from the apartheid ban. Reared by a penniless grandmother and unable to attend school, his talent for running was recognized and he was employed as a kitchen cleaner in a coal mine which wanted him in its athletics team. Still only able to speak in his Ndebele dialect he went to Atlanta ranked 41st in the world at the Marathon and the shortest runner in the field at five feet two inches. He won by three seconds. Almost as moving was the victory of Jefferson Perez of Ecuador in the 20 kilometres walk. His first name (meant to be Jersinio) was a result of a mistake by a clerk at the registry office. His victory was the first medal of any kind for Ecuador and on his return he brought traffic to a halt in the country's capital (though this is a common occurrence in Quito anyway) and he had a stadium named after him in his home town of Cuenca. And in the women's Marathon the unknown Fatuma Roba, a farmer's daughter from Ethiopia, upstaged all the favourites to win by an amazing two minutes. Britain's performance at Atlanta was disappointing, the nadir being the disqualification of Linford Christie from the 100 metres for two false starts. It was the 36-year-old's last Olympics. A fourth gold medal went to Steve Redgrave who, exhausted after the victory, asked onlookers to shoot him if they ever saw him in a boat again. However, he relented in time for Sydney, expressing disappointment with the atmosphere of the Atlanta games and lured out of a very brief retirement (all of two months) by what he described as the 'sporting culture' of Australia.

At Atlanta 197 nations were represented by 6,797 male and 3,523 female competitors, the first time that women represented more than a third of the total.

## Sydney 2000
*Watch out for sharks!*

Despite dire warnings from predictably gloomy media, the Sydney Games were deservedly judged the best ever. It was confidently anticipated in some quarters that the facilities, particularly the transportation arrangements, would not be ready in time but as so often the media proved to be wrong. Even a widely expressed fear that competitors in the triathlon (running, cycling, swimming) would be consumed by sharks in Sydney Harbour proved to be mistaken. The sharks stayed away. The torch relay, by a circuitous route, travelled 31,811 miles and the only embarrassment occurred when it was noticed that the Olympic medals bore an image of the Colosseum in Rome: wrong country, wrong city, no gladiators. The

swimmer Eric 'the Eel' Moussambani from Equatorial Guinea achieved a moment of fame comparable with that of 'Eddie the Eagle' at Calgary when he completed the slowest ever 100 metres heat, alone, two other competitors having been disqualified. He had learned to swim eight months earlier in a 20-metre pool. To the relief of the spectators, who cheered him enthusiastically, he didn't drown. The highlight for Great Britain came when Steve Redgrave won his fifth gold medal, in a particularly gruelling race for Britain's coxless four, by the fine margin of 0.4 seconds, followed home by Italy and the hosts Australia. Another member of the crew, Tim Foster, said of the victory, 'They told me if we won it wouldn't hurt. They lied.' Steve Redgrave had been

*Steve Redgrave*

supported by his wife, a family doctor, in his sporting activities and Britain achieved another notable gold when Stephanie Cook, a medical student from Cambridge, took some time off from her medical training to win the women's inaugural Modern Pentathlon (fencing, shooting, show jumping, swimming and cross-country running).

Two gymnasts lost medals in controversial circumstances. The Romanian Andrea Raducan became the first gymnast to forfeit a medal, the gold, in the floor exercise, after being prescribed Nurofen, available in any pharmacy, by the team doctor. It contained small quantities of a prohibited substance so Raducan lost her medal (though she kept two others, a gold and silver) and the team doctor lost his job. Ten years after winning a bronze medal at Sydney the Chinese gymnast Dong Fangxiao was stripped of the medal when it was discovered that at Sydney she was only 14 years old (to be eligible athletes must be at least 16 during the Olympic year). But the greatest drugs controversy involved the US athlete Marion Jones who won five medals

in sprint events and the long jump. In 2007, after a long enquiry, she admitted taking banned substances and was stripped of her medals as were her unfortunate compatriots in the two relay events, though these were later restored after appeal.

At Sydney 200 nations were represented by 6,582 male and 4,069 female competitors.

## JACQUES ROGGE, IOC PRESIDENT, 2001-

In 2001 Jacques Rogge (born 1942), a Belgian orthopaedic surgeon, succeeded Juan Antonio Samaranch as IOC President. Of his predecessor Rogge said, 'from Juan Antonio Samaranch, I learned the politics of sport', perhaps a back-handed compliment! Unlike most of his predecessors (Avery Brundage being the exception) Rogge is himself an athlete of some distinction. He competed in yachting events at the Summer Olympics of 1968, 1972 and 1976 and played for the Belgian national rugby team. One of his declared aims is to make it possible for developing nations to host the Olympics which implies a reduction in cost and, perhaps, a reduction in the size of the event. He has had to deal with the aftermath of the Salt Lake City bribery scandal and negotiated with some difficulty the delicate matter of Chinese censorship during the Peking Games. He also dealt with an unforeseen controversy arising from the Vancouver Winter Olympics from which women's ski jumping was excluded, insisting rather unconvincingly that the decision was 'strictly on a technical basis and not on gender grounds'. This overlooked the fact that the record for the longest single jump is held by a woman, Lindsey Van. The event will be included at the Sochi Olympics in 2014.

'THE CITY OF …
LONDON'

*On 6 July 2005 Jacques Rogge brought delight to Trafalgar Square and much else of Britain by announcing that London had been chosen, by the narrow margin of 54 votes to 50 over Paris, to host the 2012 Olympics. Paris had been the favourite while Moscow, New York and Madrid were eliminated in earlier rounds. The following day, 7th July, four suicide bombers killed 52 of their fellow citizens on the London tube and bus network. How would this atrocity have affected the vote if it had taken place two days earlier?*

## Athens, 2004
*Home again*

In 2004 Athens at last regained the Olympics that it thought it would keep for ever in 1896. There was a good deal of anxiety about the preparations, not least because of the activities of a terror group calling themselves N17 who killed 23

*Athens Stadium 2004*

people over a period of 27 years. In June 2002 one of its members, Savvas Xiros, nearly killed himself with his own bomb leading to the break-up of the group two years before the Athens Olympics began. There were further worries, with some facilities being only just completed in time and a certain confusion attended the opening ceremony since the Greeks spelt out the names of the teams using the Greek alphabet (at previous Olympics, even in Tokyo, the Latin alphabet with which we are familiar had been employed). As a result the Caribbean island of St Lucia led the procession with Greece, the host nation, entering last in accordance with normal practice. The Panathenian stadium was once again brought into use. Two and a half millennia after it saw its first competitive games it was used for the archery competition and for the Marathon finish, though on this occasion the women competitors were allowed to enter the stadium, unlike Stamata Revithi in 1896. Acute embarrassment was caused when the Greek medal hopes Kostas Kenteris and Katerina Thanou attempted

to evade a drugs test by staging a motorbike accident before the Games began but after that low point the Games moved into gear.

## SALT LAKE CITY

*The intercalated Winter Games were held at Salt Lake City in the USA which had tried several times in the past to secure them but without success. The two men mostly concerned with winning the games for the city, a lawyer and a car salesman, had previously distributed Stetson hats to members of the IOC but they went further for the 2002 games, offering property, plastic surgery, holidays and scholarships. In 1998 this all came to light when a Utah television station reported that the Salt Lake organizing committee was paying the university fees of Sonia Essomba, daughter of an IOC member from Cameroon. Further revelations came from the Swiss member, Marc Hodler, leading to the expulsion of ten members of the IOC while ten others were sanctioned. Oddly, it seemed that no-one had actually broken any explicit rules. The lawyer and the car salesman were acquitted of all charges and Salt Lake City kept the games. Salt Lake City achieved a further ambiguous distinction when gold medals were awarded to both a Canadian and a Russian pair in figure skating after allegations of collusion amongst some judges.*

In the Summer Games a most undesirable 'first' occurred when the Irish horse, Waterford Crystal, tested positive for banned substances after winning the gold medal. The enquiry into the affair was hampered by the disappearance of the 'B' sample of the horse's urine and of a number of important documents. In 2005 the rider Cian O'Connor forfeited his medal. Another 'first' involved the Iranian judo competitor Arash Miresmaili who was the world featherweight champion, favourite for the gold medal and flag-bearer for Iran at the opening ceremony. He went on an eating binge the night before he was due to compete against an Israeli judoist, supposedly in protest against the IOC's recognition of the state of Israel. Consequently he was banned from the featherweight

division in which he was supposed to compete but congratulated and rewarded by Iran. However, he subsequently fell out with the regime of Mahmoud Ahmadinejad by supporting his opponent in the controversial presidential elections of 2009 and has been virtually banned from participation in the sport in Iran.

At Athens 201 nations were represented by 6,582 male and 4,069 female competitors.

# Beijing 2008
*Birds Nests and 're-education through labour'*

The main talking points of the Beijing Olympics of 2008 were the polluted air of the Chinese capital, human rights problems in China and

*Birds Nest Stadium*

the striking design of the stadium which resembled a bird's nest, more often associated with Chinese soup than athletics. Human rights and the stadium came together in the person of the artist Ai Weiwei who was involved in the stadium's design and jailed by the authorities, supposedly for financial irregularities but in reality for protesting about human rights. The protests began before the Olympics when the ceremony of lighting the torch at Olympia was disrupted by protesters brandishing a flag which carried the Olympic rings shown as handcuffs. Those bearing the torch in the relay from Olympia to China were attacked on several occasions, notably in Paris, one of the themes being Chinese oppression in Tibet. The Chinese authorities announced that 'protest permits' would be issued to those wishing to demonstrate but later reported that, of 77 applications, 74 were withdrawn, two suspended and one disallowed! Unofficial protests from Chinese citizens whose homes were demolished to make way for the Olympic facilities were met with jail terms for 'disturbing social order'

or, in the case of two women in their late 70s, suspended sentences of 're-education through labour'. The loudest protest by far came from the film director Steven Spielberg who stepped down from his role as artistic director of the opening ceremony because the Chinese government refused to exert any pressure on the government of Sudan to prevent the 'crimes against humanity' which the Khartoum regime was carrying out in the Darfur region. The problem of air pollution was overcome by closing down factories for the duration of the games and allowing motorists to drive on alternate days only, depending upon whether the number of their licence plate was odd or even. The press became agitated when they learned that the young Chinese girl who sang 'Ode to the Motherland' at the opening ceremony was lip-synching to a recording made by another voice but the excitement subsided when it was observed that the celebrated Luciano Pavarotti had lip-synched at the opening of the Turin Winter Olympics.

## TURIN 2006

*Following the Salt Lake City scandal a different selection process was used for the 2006 Winter Games, IOC members being denied permission to visit candidate cities except as part of an IOC delegation. A 'Selection College' made initial appraisals and produced a shortlist of two, Turin in Italy and Sion in Switzerland. To the surprise of many, Turin beat the favourite Sion and it was suggested in some quarters that this was to punish the Swiss for the role of Switzerland's Marc Hodler in 'blowing the whistle' on the Salt Lake City bribes.*

However, amongst all these difficulties there was time for some sport. The Spanish basketball teams caused controversy before the games began when the men's and women's teams posed together for a photograph in a popular Spanish newspaper, *Diario Marca*, pulling back the skin on either side of their eyes to mimic the shape of the Chinese eye. The Iranian swimmer Mohammed Alirezaei withdrew from a heat in which he was to compete with Israel's

Tom Be'eri, probably on orders from Tehran, but this was small beer compared to the boycotts that stained the games of the 1970s and 1980s. Swedish wrestler Ara Abrahamian was so annoyed at his loss to an Italian wrestler in the semi-finals of the event that, at the medal ceremony, he dropped his bronze medal to the floor after being presented with it. He was disqualified. However, his behaviour was mild compared with that of Angel Matos of Cuba who received a lifetime ban from taekwando competition after kicking the referee in the face and attacking

*Rebecca Adlington*

another official. The Games were a great success for the British team who came fourth in the medals table after China, the USA and Russia with 47 medals, of which 19 were gold. Three of the golds went to Chris Hoy in the velodrome and two to Rebecca Adlington in the swimming pool: Britain's best overall result since London 1908.

## THEY LIKE 'EM YOUNG

*Following the disqualification of Dong Fangxiao for being under-age at Sydney, doubts have been raised about the ages of two further Chinese female gymnasts, He Kexin and Jiang Yuyuan, each of whom won a gold medal. Articles in the Chinese press before the Olympics suggested that the two gymnasts were about 14 rather than the 16 years required and these claims appeared to be supported not only by the girls' childlike appearance but also by official documents which subsequently disappeared. An IOC enquiry was assured the documentation errors were the cause of the misunderstanding and no further action was taken. Not everyone was convinced.*

The economic benefits to China from the 2008 Olympics were disappointing. The number of visitors was far fewer than anticipated, almost certainly because of stringent visa restrictions which were designed to exclude potential troublemakers but which, along with adverse publicity over pollution and human rights, had the effect of excluding genuine visitors. Air China saw its passenger numbers actually fall by almost a fifth compared with the previous year and hotel occupancy rates fell as low as 40 per cent in some cases. A claim that all tickets had been sold was contradicted by the prevalence of empty seats at many events, an embarrassment only partly mitigated by bussing in local residents and cheerleaders. It was estimated that 4.7 billion people watched the Beijing Olympics at some point during the games.

At Beijing 205 nations were represented by 6,450 and 4,746 female athletes – the first time that the number of male athletes fell while the number of female competitors continued to grow.

# LONDON 2012

## London 2012
*Don't forget the newts!*

So what of London 2012? What will that add to the Olympic story? The London Olympics will certainly be the most expensive ever, with the latest estimates suggesting that the investment in facilities will amount to about £9.3 billion, compared with £732,268 for the 1948 London Games: more than 12,000 times as much. About 75,000 British firms have been involved in the work, from the major construction projects to the supply of flags and programmes, with much of the civil engineering being at the cutting edge of the profession.

*London 2012 Stadium*

Besides the challenges involved in constructing the facilities there have been some less obvious tasks to undertake including the cleansing of tens of thousands of tons of polluted soil and the transfer of 2,000 newts from the Olympic site to a nature reserve. The toughest assignment was given to the tunnellers who had to demolish 50 electricity pylons and re-route their high-tension cables through six kilometres of tunnels without interrupting the electricity supply to East London. The presence of over eight kilometres of waterways within the Olympic Park enabled much of the construction material to be brought in by narrow-boat once the canals and rivers concerned had been thoroughly cleaned of rubbish and industrial pollutants. The Olympic stadium was designed so that its top tiers could be removed after the Games, reducing the capacity from 85,000 spectators to a number suitable for a Premier Division football stadium, and the Olympic Village will be transformed into 2,800 homes, half of which will be affordable homes for people on modest incomes. The Aquatic

Centre, designed by Zaha Hadid, was built so that the 100 metre pool, with seats for 17,500 spectators, can be converted to two 50 metre pools with room for far fewer spectators so that it is better suited to community use. Four thousand trees are being planted on the site to absorb rainfall and carbon dioxide. A new school, Chobham Academy, will open on the Olympic site immediately after the Games, with places for 1,800 pupils aged three to 19 and specializing in performing arts and sport. The formerly derelict land will also accommodate Stratford's 'Westfield Centre East', echoing the Westfield Centre which occupies much of the White City site used for the 1908 London Games. It will be the largest shopping centre in Europe with 1.9 million square feet of retail space offering 14,000 jobs. Other venues will also host Olympic events, many of them with their own rich history. Cycling time trials will take place at Hampton Court, the triathlon swimming event will be in the Serpentine in Hyde Park, while Horse Guards Parade, more often associated with the annual Trooping

the Colour ceremony, will be covered in sand for the beach volleyball competition. Wembley stadium, along with other famous grounds throughout the country including Old Trafford, Manchester, the Millennium Stadium, Cardiff, and Hampden Park, Glasgow, will be used for football. Lord's cricket ground will be used for archery and Wimbledon, of course, for tennis. Rowing, in which Team GB will be hoping for a haul of medals, will take place at Lake Dorney, near Eton College, to which it belongs. The equestrian events will take place at Greenwich and sailing in Dorset at Weymouth and Portland harbour. The most prominent feature of the Olympic Park will be a sculpture by the Turner-prize winning artist Anish Kapoor. It features the five Olympic rings in a spiralling design reaching to a height of 115 metres and, from its platform, offers a panoramic view of London.

The early indications are that attendances will be very high. Nearly 9 million tickets went on sale in March 2011 of which 2.5 million cost less than £20 and in the case of young children the price of the

*Nelson's Column*

ticket will be no more than the age, in years, of the child. The Olympic torch will arrive in Britain on Friday 18 May and, after travelling around Britain for 70 days, it will arrive at the Olympic stadium in time for the Games to begin on 27 July. Exactly a year earlier, on 27 July 2011, the President of the IOC, Jacques Rogge, in a ceremony in Trafalgar Square, called upon the athletes of the world to assemble in London in 2012. Boris Johnson, the London Mayor, drew attention to the fact that the Olympic venues were ready a year in advance and proposed to call a snap Olympics

there and then! The number of nations participating is expected to be 202 and the number of athletes is expected to exceed the 11,196 who competed at Beijing, with the Village designed to accommodate 17,320 athletes and officials. In a nice touch the official mascots are to be called 'Wenlock', a tribute to the Much Wenlock Olympics of William Penny Brookes, and, for the Paralympics, the mascot will be 'Mandeville' after the hospital at Stoke Mandeville in Buckinghamshire where the Paralympics began in 1948. Two million tickets for the London Paralympics went on sale in September 2011.

In July 2011, just over a year before the London Games begin, Keri-Anne Payne became the first person officially to qualify for London 2012 when she won the 10 kilometre open water race at the world swimming championships. So who will be the British stars and medal winners at 2012? Here are just a few names:

**Rowing:** Katherine Grainger and Anna Watkins, women's double sculls; winners in the World Rowing Championships, New Zealand, 2010.

Katherine Grainger has three Olympic silver medals to her credit and seeks gold at Lake Dorney. Peter Reed and Andy Hodge, winners of gold in Britain's four at Beijing may compete as a pair or once again row in a four.

**Sailing:** at Weymouth Ben Ainslie will look for his fourth gold medal in the Finn class.

**Swimming:** Rebecca Adlington will be seeking further golds in the 400 metres and 800 metres freestyle events as will Keri-Anne Payne as reigning 10 km world champion. Ellen Gandy will be looking to improve on her silver medal in the 200 metres butterfly at the world swimming championships in Shanghai in 2011.

**Athletics:** Jessica Ennis will carry British hopes in the heptathlon event and Mo Farah will challenge the Kenyans and Ethiopians at 5,000 or 10,000 metres. If Christine Ohuruogu can avoid injury she must be a contender for the 400 metres gold.

**Cycling:** Britain's 8 golds in Beijing may be out of reach, with a determined challenge from the Australians, but Chris Hoy will be seeking to add to his tally of three golds from Beijing and one from

Athens. And keep an eye open for Jason Kenny in the sprint who will be aiming to add to his gold in the team sprint in Beijing; and also Bradley Wiggins and Mark Cavendish, the latter after becoming the first Briton to win the coveted Green Jersey as the sprint champion in the 2011 Tour de France. And Victoria Pendleton will be aiming to add to the gold she won in the sprint in Beijing.

**Gymnastics:** in a sport in which Britain has not normally excelled, hopes rest on Beth Tweddle, who has won world championships on the uneven bars and floor exercises.

It is estimated that television rights for the Summer Olympics will reach $3 billion for the first time and that another 'first' could see the worldwide TV audience exceed 5 billion viewers.

In the meantime controversy has already arisen over the choice of Sochi, in Russia, for the 2014 Winter Olympics. In August 2008 the state of Georgia in the Caucasus, Josef Stalin's birthplace, called for a boycott of Sochi because of Russian participation in the 2008 South Ossetia war. PLEASE NO!

# Index

# MORE AMAZING TITLES

## LOVED THIS BOOK?

Tell us what you think and you could win another fantastic book from David & Charles in our monthly prize draw.

www.lovethisbook.co.uk

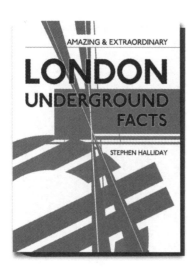

**AMAZING & EXTRAORDINARY LONDON UNDERGROUND FACTS**
Stephen Halliday
ISBN: 978-0-7153-3277-1